EDEXCEL INTERNATIONAL GCSE (9–1)

HISTORY
GERMANY: DEVELOPMENT OF DICTATORSHIP, 1918–45
Student Book

Victoria Payne

Series Editor: Nigel Kelly

Published by Pearson Education Limited, 80 Strand, London, WC2R 0RL.

www.pearsonglobalschools.com

Copies of official specifications for all Pearson qualifications may be found on the website: https://qualifications.pearson.com

Text © Pearson Education Limited 2017
Edited by Stephanie White and Sarah Wright
Designed by Cobalt id and Pearson Education Limited
Typeset and illustrated by Phoenix Photosetting Ltd, Chatham, Kent
Original illustrations © Pearson Education Limited 2017
Cover design by Pearson Education Limited
Picture research by Andreas Schindler
Cover photo/illustration **Mary Evans Picture Library:** Sueddeutsche Zeitung Photo
Inside front cover Shutterstock.com: Dmitry Lobanov

The rights of Victoria Payne to be identified as author of this work have been asserted by her in accordance with the Copyright, Designs and Patents Act 1988.

First published 2017

20 19 18
10 9 8 7 6 5 4 3 2

British Library Cataloguing in Publication Data
A catalogue record for this book is available from the British Library

ISBN 978 0 435 18538 1

Printed in Slovakia by Neografia

Acknowledgements
The author and publisher would like to thank the following individuals and organisations for permission to reproduce photographs:
(Key: b-bottom; c-centre; l-left; r-right; t-top)

akg-images Ltd: 75tr, 76cr, 84cr
Alamy Stock Photo: age fotostock 100tr, Archivart 72br, Chronicle 12br, 15tr, 42tc, ivcr, Niall Ferguson 28br, GL Archive 27cl, 44cr, Heritage Image Partnership Ltd 53bl, INTERFOTO 5br, 44tr, 44c, 44cl, 51tr, 73tr, 79bc, John Frost Newspapers 4cr, Mary Evans Picture Library vc, 46br, Pictorial Press Ltd 54br, World History Archive 97br
British Cartoon Archive, University of Kent www.cartoons.ac.uk: David Low / Solo Syndication / Associated Newspapers Ltd 67tr
Getty Images: Bettmann 34tr, Keystone 19cr, 102cr, Photo12 / UIG 60, ullstein bild 2, 24, 39, 93, Universal History Archive 14br, Universal History Archive / UIG 83tr
Mary Evans Picture Library: 30cr, 32br, 49cr, 71tc, 72tr, Punch 12tr, SZ Photo 31b, 61br, ivbl, SZ Photo / Scherl 26cr, 68br, 81br, 88br, WEIMAR ARCHIVE 25br
Museumsstiftung Post und Telekommunikation, Archiv für Philatelie: Museum Foundation Post and Telecommunication, Philatelic Archive Bonn, Germany / Bundesministerium der Finanzen 105cr

All other images © Pearson Education Limited

We are grateful to the following for permission to reproduce copyright material:

Figures
Figure on page 7 from *A GCSE History for WJEC Specification: In-Depth and Outline Studies of Aspects of Welsh/English and World History (WJEC GCSE History (COMET))*, Heinemann (Evans, R.P and Jones-Evans P. 2003) p.133, Pearson Education Limited

Text
Extract on page 7 from *Modern World History for OCR: Core Textbook: Core Edition (OCR Modern World History 2009)*, 2nd ed., Heinemann (Kelly,N. and Lacey,G.) p.100, Pearson Education Ltd; Extract on page 11 from *Weimar and the Rise of Hitler (The making of the 20th century)*, 2nd Revised ed., Macmillan (Nicholls,A.J. 1979) Macmillan Publishers Limited; Extract on page 18 from *Weimar and Nazi Germany (SHP Advanced History Core Texts)*, Reprint ed., (Hinton,C. and Hite,J. 2000) p.49, reproduced by permission of Hodder Education; Extract on page 35 from *Nationalism, dictatorship and democracy in the 20th Century Europe*, Pearson (Hall K., Shuter J., Brown D., Williams B.) Pearson Education Ltd; Extract on page 45 from *Hitler and Stalin: Parallel Lives*, Reprint ed., Vintage (Bullock,A. 1993), reprinted by permission of HarperCollins Publishers Ltd © 1992 by Alan Bullock. Also used by permission of Alfred A. Knopf, an imprint of the Knopf and Doubleday Publishing Group, a division of Penguin Random House LLC. All rights reserved; Extract on page 52 from *From Weimar to Auschwitz: Essays in German History*, Princeton University Press (Mommsen,H. 1991) Permission granted by Polity Press; Extract on page 58 from *Modern World History*, Heinemann (Kelly and Lacey 2001) p.103, Pearson Education Ltd; Extract on page 67 from *Weimar and Nazi Germany (SHP Advanced History Core Texts)* Reprint ed., Hodder Education (Hinton,C. and Hite, J. 2000) p.179, reproduced by permission of Hodder Education; Extract on page 84 from The Holocaust: A Learning Site for Students/ THE EVIAN CONFERENCE, https://www.ushmm.org/outreach/en/article.php?ModuleId=10007698, UNITED STATES HOLOCAUST MEMORIAL MUSEUM; Extract on page 95 from Holocaust Education & Archive Research Team / The Warsaw Ghetto, Copyright SJ H.E.A.R.T 2006 - 2007; Extract on page 97 from *Edexcel GCSE History B: Schools History Project - Germany Student Book (2C)*, 1 ed., Edexcel (Waugh, S. 2009) p.95, Pearson Education Limited; Extract on page 104 from War Jokes: Humor In Hitler's Germany by Rudolph Herzog with permission from the author.

Select glossary terms have been taken from *The Longman Dictionary of Contemporary English Online*.

Disclaimer
All maps in this book are drawn to support the key learning points. They are illustrative in style and are not exact representations.

Endorsement Statement
In order to ensure that this resource offers high-quality support for the associated Pearson qualification, it has been through a review process by the awarding body. This process confirms that this resource fully covers the teaching and learning content of the specification or part of a specification at which it is aimed. It also confirms that it demonstrates an appropriate balance between the development of subject skills, knowledge and understanding, in addition to preparation for assessment.

Endorsement does not cover any guidance on assessment activities or processes (e.g. practice questions or advice on how to answer assessment questions) included in the resource nor does it prescribe any particular approach to the teaching or delivery of a related course.

While the publishers have made every attempt to ensure that advice on the qualification and its assessment is accurate, the official specification and associated assessment guidance materials are the only authoritative source of information and should always be referred to for definitive guidance.

Pearson examiners have not contributed to any sections in this resource relevant to examination papers for which they have responsibility.

Examiners will not use endorsed resources as a source of material for any assessment set by Pearson. Endorsement of a resource does not mean that the resource is required to achieve this Pearson qualification, nor does it mean that it is the only suitable material available to support the qualification, and any resource lists produced by the awarding body shall include this and other appropriate resources.

CONTENTS

ABOUT THIS BOOK

This book is written for students following the Edexcel International GCSE (9–1) History specification and covers one unit of the course. This unit is Germany: Development of Dictatorship, 1918–45, one of the Depth Studies.

The History course has been structured so that teaching and learning can take place in any order, both in the classroom and in any independent learning. The book contains five chapters which match the five areas of content in the specification:

- The establishment of the Weimar Republic and its early problems
- The recovery of Germany, 1924–29
- The rise of Hitler and the Nazis to January 1933
- Nazi Germany, 1933–39
- Germany and the occupied territories during the Second World War

Each chapter is split into multiple sections to break down content into manageable chunks and to ensure full coverage of the specification.

Each chapter features a mix of learning and activities. Sources are embedded throughout to develop your understanding and exam-style questions help you to put learning into practice. Recap pages at the end of each chapter summarise key information and let you check your understanding. Exam guidance pages help you prepare confidently for the exam.

Learning objectives
Each section starts with a list of what you will learn in it. They are carefully tailored to address key assessment objectives central to the course.

Activity
Each chapter includes activities to help check and embed knowledge and understanding.

Extend your knowledge
Interesting facts to encourage wider thought and stimulate discussion. They are closely related to key issues and allow you to add depth to your knowledge and answers.

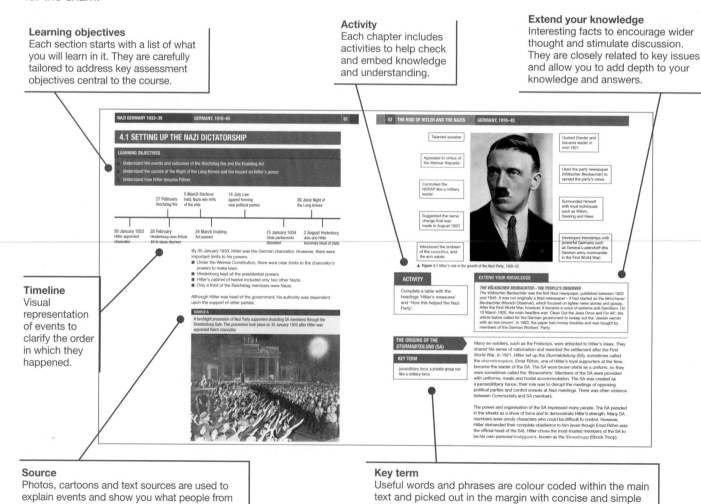

Timeline
Visual representation of events to clarify the order in which they happened.

Source
Photos, cartoons and text sources are used to explain events and show you what people from the period said, thought or created, helping you to build your understanding.

Key term
Useful words and phrases are colour coded within the main text and picked out in the margin with concise and simple definitions. These help understanding of key subject terms and support students whose first language is not English.

Exam-style question
Questions tailored to the Pearson Edexcel specification to allow for practice and development of exam writing technique. They also allow for practice responding to the command words used in the exams.

Recap
At the end of each chapter, you will find a page designed to help you consolidate and reflect on the chapter as a whole.

Recall quiz
This quick quiz is ideal for checking your knowledge or for revision.

Skills
Relevant exam questions have been assigned the key skills which you will gain from undertaking them, allowing for a strong focus on particular academic qualities. These transferable skills are highly valued in further study and the workplace.

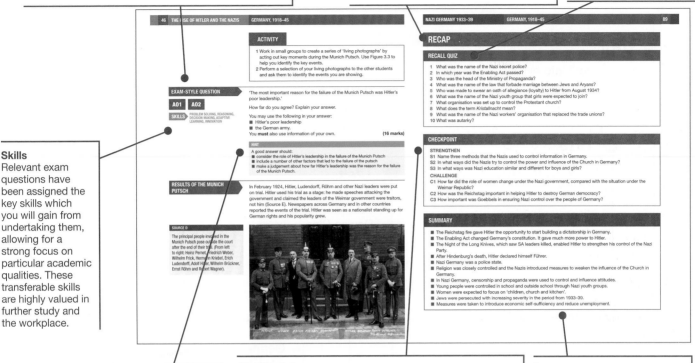

Hint
All exam-style questions are accompanied by a hint to help you get started on an answer.

Checkpoint
Checkpoints help you to check and reflect on your learning. The Strengthen section helps you to consolidate knowledge and understanding, and check that you have grasped the basic ideas and skills. The Challenge questions push you to go beyond just understanding the information, and into evaluation and analysis of what you have studied.

Summary
The main points of each chapter are summarised in a series of bullet points. These are great for embedding core knowledge and handy for revision.

Exam guidance
At the end of each chapter, you will find two pages designed to help you better understand the exam questions and how to answer them. Each exam guidance section focuses on a particular question type that you will find in the exam, allowing you to approach them with confidence.

Student answers
Exemplar student answers are used to show what an answer to the exam question may look like. There are often two levels of answers so you can see what you need to do to write better responses.

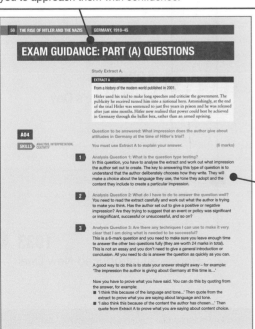

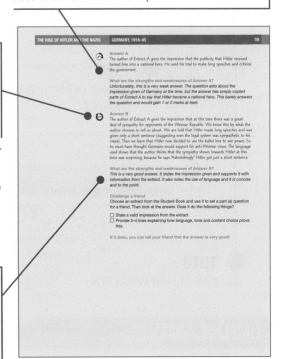

Pearson progression
Sample student answers have been given a Pearson step from 1 to 12. This tells you how well the response has met the criteria in the Pearson Progression Map.

Advice on answering the question
Three key questions about the exam question are answered here in order to explain what the question is testing and what you need to do to succeed in the exam.

Commentary
Feedback on the quality of the answer is provided to help you understand their strengths and weaknesses and show how they can be improved.

TIMELINE – GERMANY, 1918–45

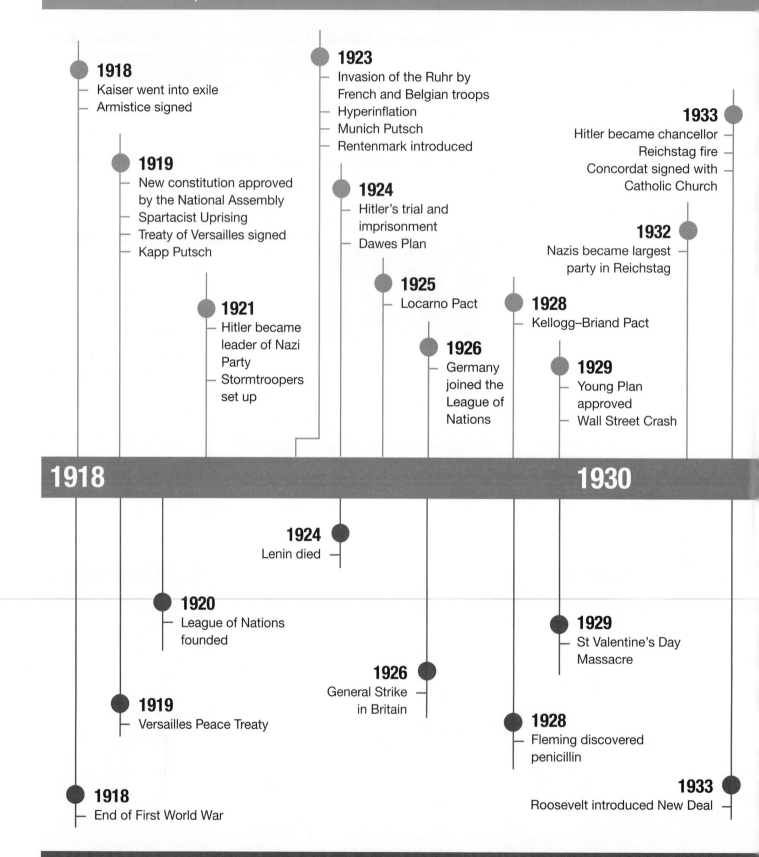

1918
— Kaiser went into exile
— Armistice signed

1919
— New constitution approved by the National Assembly
— Spartacist Uprising
— Treaty of Versailles signed
— Kapp Putsch

1921
— Hitler became leader of Nazi Party
— Stormtroopers set up

1923
— Invasion of the Ruhr by French and Belgian troops
— Hyperinflation
— Munich Putsch
— Rentenmark introduced

1924
— Hitler's trial and imprisonment
— Dawes Plan

1925
— Locarno Pact

1926
— Germany joined the League of Nations

1928
— Kellogg–Briand Pact

1929
— Young Plan approved
— Wall Street Crash

1932
— Nazis became largest party in Reichstag

1933
— Hitler became chancellor
— Reichstag fire
— Concordat signed with Catholic Church

1918

1930

1924
— Lenin died

1920
— League of Nations founded

1919
— Versailles Peace Treaty

1926
— General Strike in Britain

1929
— St Valentine's Day Massacre

1928
— Fleming discovered penicillin

1918
— End of First World War

1933
— Roosevelt introduced New Deal

TIMELINE – WORLD

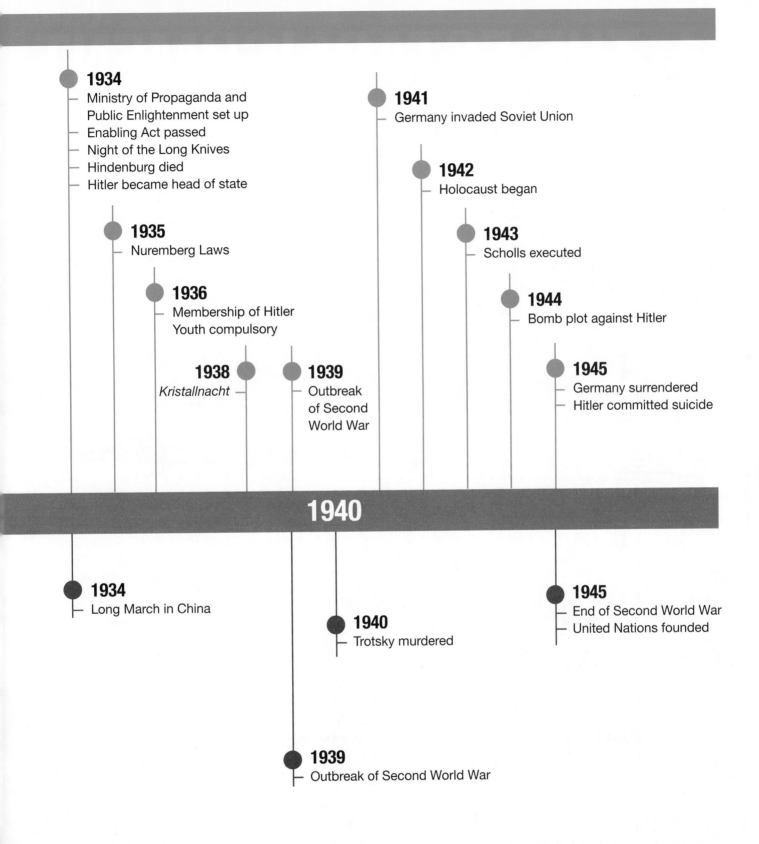

1934
Ministry of Propaganda and
Public Enlightenment set up
Enabling Act passed
Night of the Long Knives
Hindenburg died
Hitler became head of state

1935
Nuremberg Laws

1936
Membership of Hitler
Youth compulsory

1938
Kristallnacht

1939
Outbreak
of Second
World War

1941
Germany invaded Soviet Union

1942
Holocaust began

1943
Scholls executed

1944
Bomb plot against Hitler

1945
Germany surrendered
Hitler committed suicide

1940

1934
Long March in China

1940
Trotsky murdered

1945
End of Second World War
United Nations founded

1939
Outbreak of Second World War

1. THE ESTABLISHMENT OF THE WEIMAR REPUBLIC AND ITS EARLY PROBLEMS

LEARNING OBJECTIVES

- Understand the situation in Germany at the end of the First World War and the impact of the Treaty of Versailles
- Understand the strengths and weaknesses of the new German Republic and the challenges it faced
- Understand Germany's economic problems 1918–23.

When Germany finally surrendered in November 1918, many German soldiers could not believe it: they had been led to believe that they were winning the war. Between 1918 and 1919, Germany experienced a chain of events that historians call the German Revolution. During this period, the Kaiser abdicated and a new way of governing was introduced. This was a 'republic', a form of government without a monarch. A new constitution was also drawn up to show how governments were chosen in the republic and how they should carry out their work. At the end of the First World War, Germany was in chaos. The strain of the war had damaged Germany and people showed their unhappiness through strikes and protests. Many people in Germany, especially ex-soldiers, hated the new republic and everything it stood for. The consequences of the First World War meant that Germany was in economic and political difficulties. Economic problems created by the war had to be dealt with and by 1923 Germany faced a hyperinflation crisis. This further increased anger towards the Weimar Republic – some people felt the government was not able to solve Germany's problems and make Germany strong again.

1.1 THE ABDICATION OF THE KAISER AND THE ESTABLISHMENT OF THE WEIMAR REPUBLIC

LEARNING OBJECTIVES

- Understand the key features and causes of the German Revolution in 1918
- Understand the importance of the abdication of Wilhelm II
- Understand the strengths and weaknesses of the Weimar Constitution.

6 November 1918 Soldiers' and workers' councils established in some German cities

10 November 1918 Council of People's Representatives took control in Germany

January 1919 First elections were held for the Weimar parliament

25 October 1918 Naval commanders at Kiel ordered sailors to fight, leading to mutiny

9 November 1918 Kaiser went into exile in Holland

11 November 1918 The armistice was signed

31 July 1919 A new constitution was approved by the National Assembly

THE GERMAN REVOLUTION

The war had caused terrible suffering among the German people. For example, there were dreadful food shortages due to low domestic production and because the Allies had imposed a naval blockade to prevent imports of food. When Germany entered the war in 1914, its leaders promised a quick victory. Instead, Germany was drawn into a long and bloody conflict against the Allies on the Western Front. By early November 1918 – after 4 years of fighting – German troops had been forced to retreat and the country faced the threat of military occupation. The Allies insisted that peace could not come until the Kaiser abdicated, but he would not agree to stand down. In late October, the naval commanders at Kiel ordered their ships to fight against British naval forces, even though it was clear they would lose. The sailors led a mutiny and refused to fight. Over the next fortnight, there were strikes and protests across Germany and other soldiers also mutinied against the army leaders. There were calls from the German people for the Kaiser to **abdicate** – many Germans blamed him for their country's defeat. The Kaiser had lost control and many ordinary Germans set up their own workers' councils rather than accepting the authority of the Kaiser's officials.

KEY TERM

abdicate when a monarch gives up the throne

EXTEND YOUR KNOWLEDGE

During the First World War, Germany mobilised about 11 million military personnel. It is estimated that around 1.8 million were killed, while a further 1 million were taken as prisoners of war or reported as missing. Around 4 million soldiers were injured, many of whom were left with permanent physical and psychological disabilities. In addition, approximately 750,000 civilians died during the war from the effects of starvation and disease, including a flu epidemic.

THE KAISER ABDICATES

KEY TERM

armistice agreement that stops the fighting in a war

On 9 November 1918, the Kaiser finally accepted that he could not continue to rule. He abdicated and fled to Holland to live in exile. On 10 November, a new republic was set up and a new president took office – the Social Democrat, Friedrich Ebert. The next day, an **armistice** was agreed by Germany and the Allies. Ebert's representative, Matthias Erzberger, signed the armistice to officially end the First World War.

SOURCE A

Kaiser Wilhelm II abdicates, as reported on the front page of a British newspaper on 10 November 1918.

Senior members of the German armed forces claimed that Germany had been close to victory and that the surrender was unnecessary. This was not true, but many Germans chose to believe it and would not accept that Germany had lost the war. To these people, the politicians who signed the armistice were traitors. This theory was known as the 'stab in the back' and helps to explain why the new republic was so unpopular from the beginning.

ACTIVITY

1 Why do you think some Germans refused to admit that the country's armed forces had been defeated in the war?
2 Why was the Weimar Republic unpopular from the start?

EXTEND YOUR KNOWLEDGE

MATTHIAS ERZBERGER

On 26 August 1921, Erzberger was on vacation in the Black Forest. During a walk, he was shot dead by two former marine officers, who were members of the Organisation Consul (an ultra-nationalist group).

The murderers fled abroad but later returned to Germany, when the government granted amnesty for all crimes committed in 'the fight for national uprising'. Many people regarded Erzberger's assassination as a 'national act of heroism'.

THE WEIMAR REPUBLIC

After the Kaiser's abdication, a Council of People's Representatives took control of Germany in November 1918. This was a temporary measure until a new permanent government system could be put in place. Ebert promised national elections for a new National Assembly. The elections were held on 19 January 1919 and the results were positive for those promoting Germany's new democracy. The electoral turnout was high – 82 per cent of the electorate voted – and moderate parties gained most of the seats. Ebert's SDP won 40 per cent of the seats.

The new system of government did not include a kaiser or any other form of monarch. It was a republic. Since the National Assembly first met in Weimar (Berlin was too dangerous at this time), the system of government became known as 'the Weimar Republic' and the constitution the Assembly drew up is often referred to as the 'Weimar Constitution'.

KEY TERM

parliamentary democracy a system of government in which people elect representatives to a parliament to make laws and govern the country

The Weimar Constitution guaranteed every German citizen freedom of speech and religion, and equality under the law. All men and women over the age of 20 were given the vote. It set up a **parliamentary democracy** in which the elected Reichstag (parliament) made the laws and appointed the government. The head of the government was the **chancellor**. He was elected every 7 years and he could use his powers to provide checks and balances to the Reichstag. In addition, the Weimar Republic consisted of 18 states, organised as a federation. This meant that each state had its own parliament, passed its own laws and ran its own police force.

EBERT'S APPROACH

Kept state running smoothly by keeping civil servants from previous government and telling them to work with the new workers' and soldiers' councils

Reassured industry leaders that the new government would not take state control over private industries

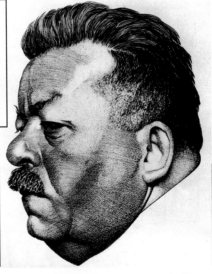

Promised trade unions that the new republic would try to reduce working hours to an 8-hour day

▶ **Figure 1.1** Ebert's approach to government

Ebert tried to reach out to different interest groups in Germany through a mixture of compromises and alliances. However, the new republic faced opposition from the start.

- Many of the country's senior figures, such as army leaders and judges, did not support the new democratic republic.
- Many other Germans wanted the Kaiser to return.
- People who had been influenced by the Russian Revolution in 1917 wanted a communist revolution to rid Germany of the industrialists and the traditional ruling class.

Germany remained very unstable and riots and demonstrations were common in many cities. Ebert's grip on power was not secure but, despite these problems, he managed to establish Germany's new constitution.

STRENGTHS AND WEAKNESSES OF THE NEW CONSTITUTION

Germany was in the process of moving from one style of government – the old system, under the Kaiser – to another, under the new republic. The new constitution set out the rules by which Germany would be governed under the new system. Some historians have argued that the constitution itself made it difficult for the republic to deal effectively with Germany's problems after the First World War. The main problems were as follows.

- Germany was politically divided and economically damaged. For the new system to be a success, politicians and other powerful forces in Germany would have to work together. However, there was a lack of commitment to do this.
- The system of proportional representation gave many different political views a say, which should have been positive. However, this type of political system requires co-operation and compromise and, unfortunately, Germany had no experience of running a political system in this way.

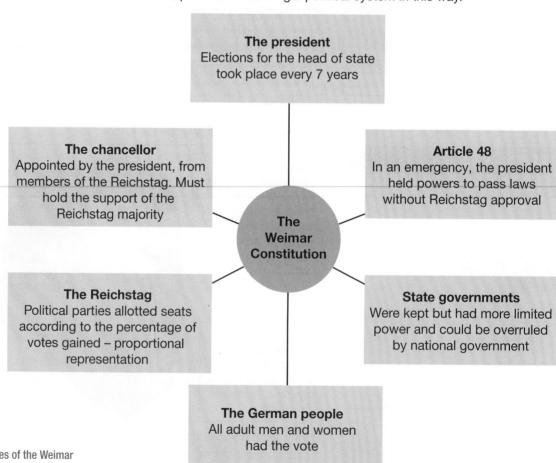

The president
Elections for the head of state took place every 7 years

The chancellor
Appointed by the president, from members of the Reichstag. Must hold the support of the Reichstag majority

Article 48
In an emergency, the president held powers to pass laws without Reichstag approval

The Weimar Constitution

The Reichstag
Political parties allotted seats according to the percentage of votes gained – proportional representation

State governments
Were kept but had more limited power and could be overruled by national government

The German people
All adult men and women had the vote

▶ **Figure 1.2** The key features of the Weimar Constitution

PROPORTIONAL REPRESENTATION

Under the system of proportional representation, seats in the Reichstag were awarded according to the percentage of votes gained. If a party won 10 per cent of the votes, it got 10 per cent of the seats in the Reichstag. (Under the old 'first past the post' system, a party could win 10 per cent of the votes but still get no seats, if they came last in all the constituencies.)

Proportional representation can be viewed as both a strength and a weakness of the new constitution: all parties which received votes had representation in the Reichstag but, as a result, many small and sometimes **extremist** parties won seats. This led to an unstable government, because no individual party had a majority and several parties had to form a **coalition**.

Coalition governments can work well when there is agreement but, in post-war Germany, the coalitions often broke down. This meant that the government no longer had a majority in the Reichstag. As a result, there was a series of short-term governments that were unable to effectively address Germany's problems as a nation. The politicians involved were seen as unhelpful and self-interested, which led to resentment among the general public.

KEY TERM

coalition a government made up of different political parties

Extreme left		Moderate left		Centre		Moderate right		Extreme right
KPD Communists	**USPD** Independent Socialists	**SPD** Social Democrats	**DDP** Democratic Party	**ZP** Centre Party	**DVP** People's Party	**DNVP** National Party	**NSDAP** Nazis (founded 1920)

▲ **Figure 1.3** Political parties in the Weimar Republic

EXTRACT A

From a recent book on the history of Germany.

The new constitution had several built-in weaknesses. Between 1919 and 1933 there was not even a single election when one party won more than half the votes cast in elections for the Reichstag. As a result, the system of proportional representation meant that no party won more than half the seats. Consequently, whichever party formed the government was forced to rely on other, less successful, parties to form squabbling and weak coalitions. When faced with having to deal with any serious political problems, the coalitions fell apart because the different parties had different views.

EXAM-STYLE QUESTION

A04

SKILLS ANALYSIS, INTERPRETATION, CREATIVITY

Study Extract A.
What impression does the author of Extract A give about the impact of proportional representation on Germany?

You **must** use Extract A to explain your answer. **(6 marks)**

HINT

Consider the language and tone of the author when explaining the impression they give.

CHANCELLORS OF THE WEIMAR REPUBLIC, 1919–23

Many chancellors found their time in office came to a sudden end when a coalition failed. The table below shows the number of days served by each chancellor between 1919 and 1923.

CHANCELLOR	DAYS IN OFFICE
Ebert	96
Scheidemann	127
Bauer	279
Muller	86
Fehrenbach	313
Wirth	1 year 188 days
Cuno	1 year 202 days

ACTIVITY

Complete the table below to show the strengths and weaknesses of the Weimar Constitution. Use the information above, including Figure 1.2, to help you.

FEATURE	STRENGTHS	WEAKNESSES
Democratic	All people had the same rights in law, including the right to vote in democratic elections.	The republic faced serious opposition from people who did not want democracy to succeed. These people also had the right to vote, so they were able to vote for parties that wanted to destroy the democratic system.
President's role	A strong president could protect the country in times of crisis.	
Chancellor's role	The chancellor needed a majority in the Reichstag, so their appointment was democratic.	
Proportional representation		Proportional representation led to many small political parties in parliament. No single party could get a majority so parties had to form coalitions. This led to weak and unstable government.
Article 48	In times of unrest, this could be used to make laws so that government could continue.	
States' rights		Individual states could oppose the national government and try to remove it.

1.2 THE TREATY OF VERSAILLES

LEARNING OBJECTIVES

- Understand the attitudes of the peacemakers at the Versailles Conference
- Understand the terms of the treaty
- Evaluate the impact of the treaty on the German people.

After the armistice was signed in November 1918, the Allies began drawing up a peace treaty. As the defeated nation, Germany expected to be punished. However, it was hopeful that the treaty would not be too harsh, for several reasons.

- Most Germans believed they had been forced into war and that all the countries involved should take responsibility.
- The Allies might want to give the new German government a chance to restore stability. A harsh treaty would make this much more difficult.
- The president of the USA, Woodrow Wilson, was a key figure in the negotiations. He was keen to make the treaty fair because he thought that harsh terms would lead to German bitterness and a desire for revenge in the longer term. In January 1918, Wilson had produced a list of 'Fourteen Points' and the Germans expected any new treaty to be based on this list.
- The Kaiser had fled and Germany had a new democratic government. Surely the Allies would not blame the new government for the actions and decisions of the Kaiser?

SOURCE B

An extract from a speech made by Georges Clemenceau at the peace conference in June 1919.

They were the first to use poisonous gas, ignoring the appalling suffering it entailed. They began the bombing and long distance shelling of towns for no military object, but solely for the purpose of reducing the morale of their opponents by striking at their women and children. They commenced the submarine campaign with its destruction of great numbers of innocent passengers and sailors, in mid ocean. They drove thousands of men and women and children with brutal savagery into slavery in foreign lands. They allowed barbarities to be practised against their prisoners of war from which the most uncivilised people would have recoiled.

However, Germany was to be disappointed: the Allies were not prepared to 'forgive and forget'. As expected, Wilson was willing to make compromises, but France and Britain had other ideas. Georges Clemenceau, the prime minister of France, was determined to make Germany pay for the terrible destruction that had occurred in France during the war (see Source B). He also wanted to weaken the German armed forces, so that France would not have to fear another attack from Germany.

The British prime minister, David Lloyd George, was keen to avoid a peace settlement that might lead to war in the future. However, he also had reasons to make sure Germany was not let off lightly. In December 1918, his government had won an election in Britain; during their campaign, they had promised to 'squeeze the German lemon until the pips squeak'. Some people in Britain even wanted to see the Kaiser hanged.

The peace treaty was known as the Treaty of Versailles. Under the terms of the treaty, the Germans had to give up land, both in Germany and overseas (as shown in Figure 1.4).

- Alsace and Lorraine were lost to France.
- Eupen and Malmedy were lost to Belgium.
- Posen and West Prussia were lost to Poland.
- Upper Silesia voted to become part of Poland.
- Northern Schleswig voted to become part of Denmark.
- The German port of Danzig was made an international city, not governed by Germany.

Overall, Germany lost about 13 per cent of its European territory; as a result, it lost almost 50 per cent of its iron reserves and 15 per cent of its coal reserves. In addition, Germany lost all 11 of its **colonies** in Africa and the Far East. These colonies were given to victorious countries as 'mandates' – territories to look after.

▶ **Figure 1.4** The territorial terms of the Treaty of Versailles

There were also non-territorial terms in the Versailles settlement.

■ Germany had to accept the blame for the war – **War Guilt**.
■ Germany had to pay **reparations** of 136,000 million marks (£6,600 million) to the Allies.
■ German military forces were cut. The main restrictions are shown in Figure 1.5.

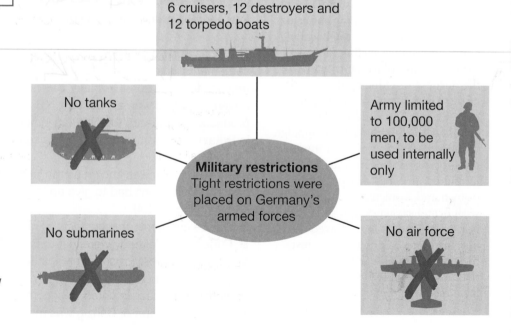

▶ **Figure 1.5** Changes to the German military force under the terms of the Treaty of Versailles

THE GERMAN REACTION TO THE TREATY

The German government was shocked by the harshness of the treaty. It had been unaware of the terms because it had not even been allowed to attend the negotiations. At first, the government refused to sign the treaty because it thought the terms were too harsh. However, the Allies threatened to restart the war if the Germans did not sign. The German politicians understood that Germany could not fight anymore – the country and the people were in a desperate state – so, reluctantly, they accepted and signed the treaty. The German representatives called the treaty a 'shameful diktat' and said they had been forced to accept terms that were unfair and deliberately humiliating.

EXTRACT B

From a recent book on the history of Germany.

Much more important than the fairness or unfairness of the treaty was its impact on the new German Republic. How far is it true that the Versailles Treaty wrecked German democracy? Much more serious was the political demoralisation which the treaty caused within Germany itself. The real damage was the disillusionment of more moderate men who might otherwise have supported the new republic.

Article 231 of the treaty (the 'War Guilt Clause') was particularly humiliating. This clause stated that Germany had to accept the blame for starting the war. The German public strongly resented this; they felt that the responsibility for the war should be shared by all the powers involved in the conflict. War guilt meant that the Allies felt justified in forcing the Germans to pay reparations, to pay for the damage caused in the war.

Many German people were angry about the government's decision to sign the treaty. They felt that Germany had been a strong and proud nation, and the Allies were deliberately seeking to weaken them. The politicians who signed the treaty were labelled the 'November Criminals' and were hated for their actions. The myth began that Germany had been stabbed in the back by its own government. Many people were determined to undermine the new government, and several politicians who argued that Germany had no choice but to sign were assassinated.

EXAM-STYLE QUESTION

AO4

SKILLS ANALYSIS, INTERPRETATION, CREATIVITY

Study Extract B.
What impression does the author of Extract B give about the impact of the Treaty of Versailles on the German people?

You **must** use Extract B to explain your answer.   **(6 marks)**

HINT

Has the author used any particular words or phrases to make an impression?

EXTEND YOUR KNOWLEDGE

FRIEDRICH EBERT
As president of Germany, Ebert was forced to accept the terms of the Versailles Treaty. However, he personally believed that the war had not really been lost and that Germany had been capable of winning. He had lost two sons who were soldiers in the war. In December 1918, he said to the German soldiers returning from war, 'Your sacrifice and deeds are without parallel. No enemy defeated you.'

EXAM-STYLE QUESTION

AO1   **AO2**

Explain **two** effects on Germany of the Treaty of Versailles.   **(8 marks)**

HINT

Remember to give two separate effects. For example, you could talk about the economic impact on Germany as a result of reparations and land losses, and the psychological impact on Germany of accepting war guilt.

SOURCE C

A cartoon from a British magazine published in 1919.

PUNCH, OR THE LONDON CHARIVARI.—April. 23, 1919.

THE RECKONING.

Pan-German. "MONSTROUS, I CALL IT. WHY, IT'S FULLY A QUARTER OF WHAT *WE* SHOULD HAVE MADE *THEM* PAY, IF WE'D WON."

SOURCE D

From a German newspaper on 28 June 1919.

Today in the Hall of Mirrors the disgraceful treaty is being signed. Do not forget it! The German people will, with unceasing labour, press forward to reconquer the place among the nations to which they are entitled.

SOURCE E

A German cartoon showing the leaders of other countries conspiring to punish Germany.

1.3 CHALLENGES TO THE WEIMAR REPUBLIC FROM LEFT AND RIGHT

LEARNING OBJECTIVES

Understand the unrest in Germany after the First World War

Understand the events and consequences of the Spartacist Uprising and the Kapp Putsch

Understand Germany's economic problems in the years 1919–23.

15 January 1919
Rosa Luxemburg killed

March 1920 Kapp Putsch

5 January 1919 Spartacist Uprising began

June 1919 Treaty of Versailles blamed Germany for the war and Allies imposed terms of the treaty

6 June 1920 Elections showed less support for moderate political parties

The first governments in the Weimar Republic faced opposition, not only from those Germans angered by the Treaty of Versailles, but by **left-wing** and **right-wing** political parties and organisations. In 1917 left-wing revolutionary activity in Russia had resulted in the overthrow of the Tsar and many people saw the poverty and discontent in Europe as an ideal opportunity to spread communism. Indeed, the Kaiser's abdication in 1918 was brought on partly by uprisings against his rule in the armed forces.

But there were equally strong feelings from many Germans with right-wing views. They did not approve of the new 'liberal and democratic' way of governing the country and wanted the return of a political system led by a powerful individual ruler like the Kaiser had been previously. Many of the people with these views held influential positions in German society, such as army leaders and judges. This would make the work of the Weimar government even harder.

The table below summarises the key features of the Left and the Right in German politics in the early 1920s.

EXTREME LEFT WING	EXTREME RIGHT WING
Believed that workers should hold political power and all people should be treated as equals	Wanted a strong authoritarian government headed by a powerful leader; sought a return of the Kaiser and the previous system
Promoted the interests of workers and argued that workers should own the land and businesses themselves	Believed in capitalism and protecting the interests of private businesses and land owners
The main left-wing political party was the Communist Party (KPD)	The main right-wing party was the National Party (DNVP)
They were inspired by the Russian Revolution of 1917 and wanted a similar revolution in Germany	They hated the Communists who had opposed the Kaiser and mutinied at the end of the First World War

From 1919, Germany was governed by a coalition of moderate parties including the Social Democrats (SPD), the Democrats (DDP) and the Centre Party (ZP). However, the elections of 6 June 1920 saw a worrying decline in support for moderates. After the elections, these three parties held only 45 per cent of the seats in the Reichstag. Both the extreme left-wing and extreme right-wing parties won about 20 per cent of seats. The remaining seats were held by smaller parties. During most of the 1920s, the moderate parties continued to form majority coalitions. However, they were constantly under attack from other parties who wanted more **radical** policies. Even before the formation of the Weimar Republic, there had been an attempt to set up a communist government in Berlin.

CHALLENGE FROM THE LEFT: THE SPARTACIST UPRISING, JANUARY 1919

KEY TERMS

demobilised (of soldiers) troops who were sent back to Germany from the battlefield at the end of the war

Freikorps an estimated 250,000 ex-soldiers who refused to give up their weapons and used violence on the streets of Germany to further their political aims

After the abdication of the Kaiser, the Spartacus League (Germany's communist party) tried to set up a communist government in Berlin. On 5 January 1919, they organised a revolt in Berlin. They occupied the headquarters of the government newspaper and telephone offices and attempted to bring about a general strike. The government found it very difficult to put down this revolt because the Treaty of Versailles had limited the number of troops in the German army. Instead, the government turned to units of volunteer soldiers, men who had been **demobilised** after the war. These soldiers were known as the **Freikorps**. They hated communism and soon ended the revolt. The communist leaders, Rosa Luxemburg and Karl Liebknecht, were shot by Freikorps fighters. Although the Sparticist Uprising had been defeated, this did not mean the end of the threat to the Weimar Republic from communism. During the 1920s, the German Communist Party was the largest in Europe (outside Russia) and it regularly won at least 10 per cent of the vote in national elections. In the November 1932 elections it won 100 seats. Throughout this period it strongly opposed the 'capitalist' governments which were elected.

SOURCE F

Rosa Luxemburg speaking at a rally in 1907.

EXTEND YOUR KNOWLEDGE

Rosa Luxemburg was a revolutionary socialist who was given the nickname 'Red Rosa'. She had an international reputation as a brilliant public speaker. She was a leading critic of the war and was imprisoned for her work distributing anti-war propaganda. In 1918, she was let out of prison and went to Berlin to lead the Spartacists.

CHALLENGE FROM THE RIGHT: THE KAPP PUTSCH, MARCH 1920

Members of the Freikorps marching into Berlin in support of the Kapp Putsch in March 1920.

nationalist a person who wants a strong country that puts its national interests before others

putsch uprising

1 Identify two similarities and two differences between the Spartacist Uprising and the Kapp Putsch. You could consider their aims, leadership, support or other features.

2 Which was the greater threat to the Weimar Republic – the Spartacists or the Kapp Putsch?

When the terms of the Treaty of Versailles were announced in January 1920, the Freikorps were among its strongest opponents. The Weimar government had agreed to reduce the number of troops in the army, from 650,000 to 100,000. Many ex-soldiers felt unable to adjust to civilian life after the end of the First World War; these men joined together to form volunteer Freikorps units. In 1920, Ebert tried to disband two Freikorps units. The Freikorps revolted, marching to Berlin and declaring Dr Wolfgang Kapp as Germany's new leader. Kapp was an extreme **nationalist** who had the support of a number of army officers. The German army refused to stop the Freikorps, as they felt sympathy for the aims of the Kapp **Putsch**.

Ebert was forced to appeal to the people for support. He moved the government out of the city and encouraged the people to go on general strike to stop the revolt. Essential supplies such as gas, water and electricity were disrupted by the strikes and soon the city was unable to function. Kapp realised that he did not have the support he would need to govern Germany. He fled to Sweden, the government returned to Berlin and the Freikorps were disbanded.

The Kapp Putsch was important because it showed that the government had little military power and could not control its own capital. However, the government did seem to have the support of the majority of the people in Berlin – or, at least, they preferred Ebert's government to Kapp's extreme right wing politics.

GERMANY'S ECONOMIC PROBLEMS

By 1918, Germany was close to **bankruptcy**, due to the cost of the First World War. The Treaty of Versailles made things even worse. The Allies insisted on huge reparations payments and, at the same time, they took away some of Germany's income-generating areas (such as the coalfields in Silesia and the Saar). The Germans struggled to make the reparations payments and asked for them to be reduced. However, the Allies had taken loans during the war, and they needed the payments from Germany so they could repay the money they owed to countries like the USA. By late 1922, Germany had failed to pay some instalments. In December 1922, it missed another payment. This led to French retaliation.

▶ **Figure 1.6** A map showing the area of Germany occupied by the French in 1923

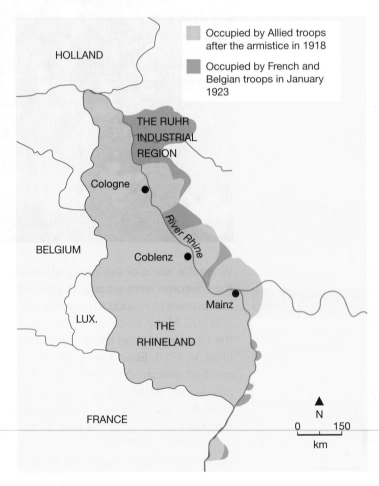

THE INVASION OF THE RUHR

In January 1923, Belgian and French troops marched into the Ruhr, the centre of Germany's production of iron, steel and coal. The Germans had fallen behind with their reparations payments and the French and Belgians decided to take industrial products instead of cash payments. The German government was angered by the invasion, but realised it could not take military action. Instead, it encouraged the workers in the Ruhr to carry out a campaign of **passive resistance**. German workers went on strike and stopped producing goods that the French could seize. Some Germans used arson and sabotage

KEY TERM

passive resistance the use of peaceful means to resist power or authority

to damage the factories and mines so that production had to stop. In response, the French brought in their own workers. There was fighting between the French and the Germans and over 100 French civilians were killed by the occupying forces. However, the occupation was profitable to France and Belgium. They did not remove their forces until July 1925, after the Dawes Plan (see page 27) was signed.

EFFECTS OF THE INVASION OF THE RUHR

The German government's reaction to the occupation of the Ruhr brought it a temporary popularity: it had resisted France and provided strike pay for the workers involved in passive resistance. The occupation also united the German nation against the invading French and Belgians.

However, the occupation had considerable negative effects. The German economy had been struggling before 1923 and the invasion of the Ruhr made things even worse. Germany lost income as a result of France and Belgium taking industrial products from the Ruhr and the German government was forced to print more money to pay the striking workers. The more notes were printed, the more their value fell and Germany entered a period of **hyperinflation**.

KEY TERM

hyperinflation extreme inflation, when prices rise very quickly

---

HYPERINFLATION, 1923

CAUSES

In the years 1919–23, the income of the German government was only one quarter of what it needed. The government decided to print more banknotes, so that it had enough money. By 1923, the government had 300 paper mills and 200 printing shops whose only job was to print money.

Unfortunately, at this time most countries linked the value of their banknotes with gold. If the German government has 10 million marks' worth of gold in its banks, it should have 10 million marks' worth of banknotes in circulation. If there are more banknotes in circulation, their value drops and prices rise dramatically. For example, if there are 20 million marks' worth of banknotes in circulation, each banknote is worth half as much – so that the total value of the banknotes still adds up to 10 million marks (to match the value of the gold).

This happened in Germany in 1923. The government had started to print more money during the First World War, to pay for the cost of the war. After it lost the war, it printed even more money so that it could pay the reparations demanded by the Treaty of Versailles. After the invasion of the Ruhr, it was forced to print yet more money, to pay the striking workers.

The table below shows the value of the German mark compared to the dollar. This shows clearly that the value of the mark dropped dramatically between 1914 and 1923.

DATE	EVENT	NUMBER OF MARKS NEEDED TO BUY 1 DOLLAR
1914	Outbreak of First World War	4
1919	German government begins to print money to pay reparations	19
1921	German economy suffering; government prints more money	65
1922	German government continues to print money	493
Jan 1923	French occupy Ruhr; government prints more money to pay striking workers	17,972
Nov 1923	German government loses income and prints more money	4.2 billion

The table below shows the number of marks needed to buy a loaf of bread in Berlin between 1918 and 1923. This too shows how the value of the mark dropped in this period.

DATE	NUMBER OF MARKS NEEDED TO BUY A LOAF OF BREAD
Dec 1918	0.54
Dec 1921	0.39
Dec 1922	163.5
Jan 1923	250
Mar 1923	463
Jun 1923	1,465
Jul 1923	3,465
Aug 1923	69,000
Sep 1923	1,512,000
Oct 1923	1,743,000,000
Nov 1923	201,000,000,000

EXTRACT A

From a recent history book about Germany.

Foreign governments must also share some blame for the crisis. The French and Belgian occupation of the Ruhr in January 1923 came as the final blow to the already weak German Mark. However it is not so much the invasion itself as the government's response to it that let loose hyperinflation.

EXAM-STYLE QUESTION

A01　**A02**

SKILLS PROBLEM SOLVING, REASONING, DECISION MAKING, ADAPTIVE LEARNING, INNOVATION

'The most important cause of the hyperinflation crisis was the French occupation of the Ruhr.'

How far do you agree? Explain your answer.

You may use the following in your answer:
- the French occupation of the Ruhr
- reparations.

You **must** also use information of your own.　　　**(16 marks)**

HINT

The bullet points are prompts to help you think about relevant information you can include in your answer. Remember that you are instructed to use information of your own, so you need to think of another factor to add to reparations and the French occupation.

SOURCE H

Children making kites out of banknotes in 1923.

EXTRACT B

From a recent book on the history of Germany.

A German landowner bought a herd of valuable cows on credit. After a while he sold one of the cows. Because the mark had deteriorated so much, the price he got for the single cow was enough to pay off the whole cost of the herd.

SOURCE I

The memories of a woman who lived in Germany during the period of hyperinflation.

A friend of mine was in charge of the office that had to deal with the giving out of... pensions... in the district around Frankfurt... One case which came her way was the widow of a policeman who had died early, leaving four children. She had been awarded three months of her husband's salary (as a pension). My friend worked out the sum with great care... and sent the papers on as required to Wiesbaden. There they were checked, rubber stamped and sent back to Frankfurt. By the time all this was done, and the money finally paid to the widow, the amount she received would only have paid for three boxes of matches.

EFFECTS

The German people were not so concerned by the falling value of the mark compared with other currencies. The real problem for them was that this fall in value led to rapid price increases, called hyperinflation. Prices rose so rapidly that, in some cases, customers in restaurants, who had enough money to pay for their meal when they sat down, did not have enough money to pay for it by the time they had finished eating!

Hyperinflation forced millions of Germans into poverty. People on fixed incomes (who received the same amount of money each week or month) – such as pensioners – were affected most badly. Soon, their income was almost worthless. The value of people's savings or insurance policies was also wiped out almost overnight. Many people who had thought they were financially secure suddenly found themselves struggling.

For people in work, the situation was not so bad, because their wages rose as well. However, the increases in wages were always slower than the price rises. Some workers took their wages and immediately used them to buy things. They could then swap these items for the things they really needed.

Some groups benefited from the hyperinflation crisis.
- People with loans and mortgages (loans used to buy houses) could pay them off much more quickly, because the real value of the loan had fallen so much (see Extract B). This helped some businesses, as they were able to pay off their business loans quickly.
- People who owned possessions, such as land or buildings, were generally protected as the value of these possessions rose in line with inflation.
- Most farmers benefited, because the food they produced could be sold at higher prices (although, of course, the things they had to buy also cost more).

Although a small number of Germans were able to benefit, hyperinflation was a disaster for Germany. Millions of **middle-class** Germans were thrown into poverty; they blamed the Weimar government for their problems (even though these problems had started before the Weimar Republic was formed). People were desperate and there was a real danger that the government might be overthrown if the country's economic problems were not resolved.

RECAP

RECALL QUIZ

1 Which countries were the Allies in the First World War?
2 On what date did Kaiser Wilhelm II abdicate?
3 Who was elected as the first president of the new Weimar Republic?
4 When was the Treaty of Versailles signed?
5 Who were the leaders of the Spartacists?
6 Which industrial region was invaded by the French in 1923?
7 What name is given to the peaceful opposition that the Germans used in response to the French occupation of their industrial heartland?
8 Who paid the strike pay for German workers during the period of their opposition?
9 What is hyperinflation?
10 Identify one benefit and one problem of hyperinflation.

CHECKPOINT

STRENGTHEN
S1 How did the 'stab in the back' theory develop?
S2 The German government caused hyperinflation by printing money. Why didn't they stop printing extra money?
S3 Identify three effects of the hyperinflation crisis, 1923.

CHALLENGE
C1 How far was proportional representation a problem for the new Weimar Republic?
C2 Why were the German people hopeful that the peace settlement in 1919 would be reasonable?
C3 Why were groups like the Freikorps so opposed to the Treaty of Versailles?

SUMMARY

- In 1918, Kaiser Wilhelm abdicated and Germany experienced a revolution in which a new political system was established.
- The new Weimar Republic was run as a democracy, which meant many changes for Germany.
- The Weimar Republic established a new constitution but it had weaknesses as well as strengths.
- The Treaty of Versailles was hugely resented by the German people who believed it was harsh and unfair on Germany.
- The new democratic politicians were blamed for the Treaty of Versailles and this weakened the prospects for the new Germany.
- Various political groups from the Left and Right did not want the new republic to survive; some groups actively tried to destabilise the new government and start revolutions.
- Germany suffered terrible economic problems in the period 1919–23. In 1923, a chain of events led to the hyperinflation crisis. The economic problems made it harder for the new Weimar Republic to become popular.

EXAM GUIDANCE: PART (C) QUESTIONS

A01 **A02**

SKILLS PROBLEM SOLVING, REASONING, DECISION MAKING, ADAPTIVE LEARNING, INNOVATION

Question to be answered: 'The main reason for the weakness of the Weimar Republic in the years 1919–23 was the Treaty of Versailles.'

How far do you agree? Explain your answer.

You may use the following in your answer:
■ the Treaty of Versailles
■ proportional representation.
You **must** also use information of your own.

(16 marks)

1 Analysis Question 1: What is the question type testing?
In this question, you have to demonstrate that you have knowledge and understanding of the key features and characteristics of the period studied. In this particular case, you need to show your knowledge and understanding of the Weimar Republic and the reasons why it was unpopular and unstable in the years up to 1923.

2 Analysis Question 2: What do I have to do to answer the question well?
■ You have been given two topics to write about – the Treaty of Versailles and proportional representation. You don't have to use the stimulus material provided, but you will find it difficult to assess the influence of the Treaty of Versailles if you don't write about it!
■ The question also says that you must include information of your own. This means that you need to include at least one other factor, as well as the two you have been given. For example, you could talk about the impact of the Freikorps.
■ Make sure you do not simply give information. Think about how the things you write about affected the Weimar Republic.
■ The question asks whether the Treaty of Versailles was the main reason for the failures of the Weimar Republic, so you must compare the reasons you write about and make a judgement about which one was most important.

3 Analysis Question 3: Are there any techniques I can use to make it very clear that I am doing what is needed to be successful?
This is a 16-mark question so you need to make sure you give a substantial answer. Try using these techniques to help you succeed.
■ Only give a brief introduction, which answers the question straight away and shows what your paragraphs are going to be about.
■ Try to use the words of the question at the beginning of each paragraph. This will help you to stay focused and avoid writing narrative.
■ Remember this is a causation question. Make sure your answer explains why the Weimar Republic struggled in the years up to 1923.
■ Don't simply state which factor was most important. Make sure you explain your choice by comparing the different factors.

In summary, to score high marks on this question, you need to do three things:
■ provide coverage of content range (at least three factors)
■ provide coverage of arguments for and against the statement in the question
■ provide clear reasons (criteria) for an overall judgement, backed by convincing argument.

Answer

Here is a student response to the question. The teacher has made some comments.

Good introduction →

The first 4 years of the Weimar Republic were very unstable, politically and economically. The terms of the Treaty of Versailles, signed in France in 1919, were harsh and very unpopular in Germany. The new Weimar government was blamed for accepting the treaty, and this was certainly a factor in making the new republic unpopular with many Germans. However, there are other factors as well, particularly the attitudes and actions of the right-wing nationalists in Germany who were determined to make democracy fail.

Good information, but this doesn't explain why the treaty caused problems for the Weimar Republic. →

The terms of the Treaty of Versailles were seen as harsh and unfair by the people of Germany. Their nation was punished and humiliated by the terms that the Allies insisted on. Germany lost her colonies and a lot of other territory where German speakers lived. Their long-standing national rival, France, was determined to make Germany pay and keen to see Germany weakened — both economically and militarily — to prevent a war of revenge. The reparations were high and Germany was in financial crisis; the government did not have the money it needed to make the economy strong again.

This is good detail, but you haven't explicitly stated whether the Treaty of Versailles led to the failures of the Weimar Republic. You have just suggested this. →

The Weimar politicians who signed the treaty were forced to do so. By November 1918, Germany could no longer continue fighting the war — the military strength of the Allies was too great after the USA joined the war in 1917. The Allies threatened to restart the fighting if the German politicians refused to sign the treaty. Furthermore, Germany was not allowed to join the negotiations or talks about the treaty. They were simply told the terms. The new socialist government was very reluctant to accept the treaty, because they knew it was too harsh.

This paragraph mentions how the system of proportional representation affected the views of the people in the Reichstag. Could you also mention some of the other parties and explain why PR made things difficult for the Weimar government? →

However, there were definitely other factors that led to the failure of the Weimar Republic, as well as the Treaty of Versailles. Proportional representation meant that the system was highly democratic. This allowed lots of parties to have representatives in the Reichstag. Many of these representatives were not democrats and some actually wanted to see the new republic collapse, so it could be replaced with a more authoritarian style of government similar to that under the Kaiser.

Good concise finish, but the paragraphs above aren't always linked back to the problems of the Weimar Republic. It is a shame that you haven't mentioned any information of your own. →

In conclusion, the Weimar Republic was weak from the outset because the problems it needed to overcome were huge. The country had a massive war debt and the losses of the war were devastating for Germany. The Allies wanted Germany to pay the price — in every sense — for losing the war. The new republic was a modern and politically advanced system but lots of ordinary people, as well as many who had traditionally been powerful in Germany, did not support the new democracy and wanted it to fail as quickly as possible.

What are the strengths and weaknesses of this answer?

You can see the strengths and weaknesses of this answer from what the teacher says. It is a fairly good answer but the student has not included any information of their own and they need to link back to the question more effectively.

Work with a friend

Discuss with a friend how you would rewrite the weaker paragraphs to enable the whole answer to get high marks.

2. THE RECOVERY OF GERMANY, 1924–29

LEARNING OBJECTIVES

- Understand the economic policies used to stabilise Germany's currency
- Understand the measures taken to reduce reparations payments through the Dawes Plan (1924) and the Young Plan (1929)
- Understand Stresemann's foreign policy achievements.

The period 1923–29 is sometimes called the 'Stresemann Era', named after the politician Gustav Stresemann. In 1923, the Weimar Republic was in crisis. Thanks to Stresemann's economic and diplomatic policies, Germany emerged from this crisis in a much healthier position. Stresemann believed it was vital to improve Germany's relations with other countries, so he could negotiate more realistic reparations payments. He hoped this would give Germany a chance to sort out its economic problems. Stresemann's approach relied on finding a way to co-operate with the Allies. He also worked hard to bring the more extreme sections of German society to a more moderate position. This allowed him to build a new, stronger Germany.

2.1 THE WORK OF GUSTAV STRESEMANN – AT HOME

LEARNING OBJECTIVES

- Understand how the introduction of the Rentenmark helped to end the currency crisis
- Understand the aims and outcomes of the Dawes Plan and the Young Plan
- Understand the role of US loans and the recovery of the German economy.

GUSTAV STRESEMANN AND THE GREAT COALITION GOVERNMENT 1923

In 1923, Germany was in crisis. This was due to the effects of hyperinflation and the French occupation of the Ruhr. Within the next few years, however, the Weimar Republic overcame its economic problems, social unrest and political revolutions and entered an age of stability and prosperity.

Much of the credit for this recovery must go to Gustav Stresemann. He became chancellor in 1923 and led the 'Great Coalition' government. This government helped to solve the urgent problem of hyperinflation and brought about important improvements in the state of the economy – for example, a fall in unemployment, more house building and investment in transport systems. Stresemann was chancellor for just 4 months, before becoming foreign secretary. He held this position until his death in October 1929.

SOURCE A

Gustav Stresemann (centre front) was chancellor of the Great Coalition government, 1923.

THE RENTENMARK

As a result of the 1923 hyperinflation crisis, the German mark was worthless. Stresemann needed to stabilise the value of the currency. In November 1923, he introduced a new currency as a temporary solution. This currency was known as the **Rentenmark** and the amount of money printed was tightly controlled.

Stresemann based the value of the Rentenmark on Germany's industrial and agricultural worth. He also promised to exchange the notes for shares in German land or industry if the currency failed. This gave the German people confidence in the new currency.

In 1924, a new independent national bank – called the **Reichsbank** – was handed control of the new currency. In the same year, the **Reichsmark** was issued to replace the Rentenmark. The Reichsmark was a new permanent currency that people in Germany and in other countries could now rely on. These measures restored faith in Germany's financial system and were vital in allowing Germany's economy to grow stronger.

SOURCE B

A pile of Rentenmark stored in the basement of the Reichsbank in 1923.

ACTIVITY

Draw a flowchart to show how Stresemann stabilised the German currency after the hyperinflation crisis.

US LOANS AND GERMAN ECONOMIC RECOVERY

Stresemann believed that Germany's economy could not recover until the issue of reparations had been solved. He argued that Germany should accept the Treaty of Versailles to improve foreign relations with Britain and France. This was a very unpopular view as most Germans hated the treaty. However, Stresemann also believed it would be possible to negotiate better terms for Germany. The USA, France and Britain had a lot to gain from allowing the German economy to recover. The USA had lent millions of dollars to France and Britain as war loans during the First World War. If the German economy improved, Germany would be able to make its reparations payments; this in turn would provide Britain and France with the money they needed to repay the USA. The Allies would also benefit if Germany was able to become a strong trading partner again.

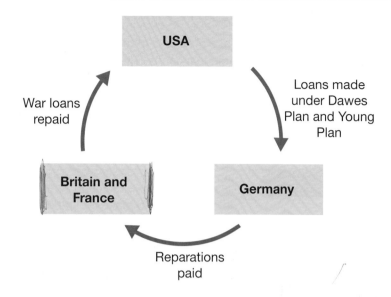

▶ **Figure 2.1** Loans and repayments between Germany and the Allies

THE DAWES PLAN 1924

Stresemann was right to believe there was a chance to negotiate better terms for reparations payments. In 1923, the USA sent Charles Dawes to Germany to help resolve its economic problems. Dawes advised Stresemann on the establishment of the Reichsbank. France and Britain accepted that Germany wanted to renegotiate the reparations payments and, in 1924, the Dawes Plan was agreed between Germany and the Allies. The key points of the Dawes Plan were as follows.

- The USA loaned Germany 800 million gold marks; this gave a massive boost to German industry.
- Reparations payments were lowered to 1,000 million marks for the first 5 years, to make them more affordable. After this time, the payments would be increased to 2,500 million marks.
- The Allies agreed to review the payment rate over time, to take account of Germany's economic situation and ability to pay.
- The French agreed to **withdraw** troops from the Ruhr. They also agreed that any missed payments in the future would be dealt with by the Allies together.
- The Allies were given some control of the Reichsbank and the railways in Germany.

Some Germans criticised the government for agreeing to the terms of the Dawes Plan. They felt that Germany was accepting the blame for starting the war by agreeing to continue with reparations payments. However, the Dawes Plan helped to restore Germany's economy and led to further loans from the USA. Over the next 6 years, Germany received more than 25 billion marks in loans. This money allowed German industry to recover.

SOURCE C

Charles Dawes.

THE EXTENT OF ECONOMIC RECOVERY

Germany's economy recovered significantly after 1924. The stability in Germany's currency meant that there was more investment in Germany from other countries, especially the USA. Much of that investment was in boosting industry and building factories. The Dawes Plan helped boost industrial output which doubled in the years 1923–29. Wages rose, the cost of living went down and the standard of living improved. Confidence in the economy was restored and the government was able to build new roads, schools and public buildings. The improvements in the economy meant that by 1927 new laws could be introduced to allow people to claim unemployment benefit and 'labour exchanges' were set up to help people still unemployed to find work.

However, foreign investment left the German economy open to risks if there were problems in the world economy. The recovery was based largely on American loans. These loans were invested in projects that would create wealth and allow the loans and interest to be paid off. What would happen if there was a downturn in the world economy? By 1927 there were signs that the German economy was slowing down and the farming industry was beginning to struggle. When the Wall Street Crash came in 1929, the Germans found out how weak their economy still was.

THE YOUNG PLAN 1929

Despite the Dawes Plan and American loans, the German government still did not find it easy to make reparations payments.

- The total reparations bill was reduced to around $8 billion.
- The payments were to be made over 59 years, at a rate of $473 million per year.
- Germany was only obliged to pay a third of the annual sum each year. It should pay the rest if it could afford to do so.

At the same, the French agreed to leave the Rhineland by June 1930 – 5 years ahead of the previously agreed date of 1935. The reduction in annual payments allowed the government to reduce taxes and released funds that were used to boost the German industry and create jobs for workers.

Many people in Germany opposed the Young Plan. Some nationalist groups were angry that Germany would continue to pay reparations. They felt that the timescale for the payments was far too long and would limit Germany's progress as a nation. Alfred Hugenberg, a media businessman, organised a petition against the plan and managed to get 4 million signatures. However, when a **referendum** was held in December 1929 – allowing people to vote to accept or reject the plan – only 14 per cent voted against it.

There was also some British opposition to the Young Plan. Two **memorials** to Britons killed in the war (at Thiepval and the Menin Gate) had only recently been completed and feelings against the Germans were still strong.

EXTEND YOUR KNOWLEDGE

THE MENIN GATE
The Menin Gate is one of four memorials to the missing in Belgian Flanders. It bears the names of 54,000 missing soldiers whose remains were never found. The site of the Menin Gate was chosen because hundreds of thousands of men passed that point on their way to the trenches. It commemorates dead soldiers from the UK, Australia, Canada, South Africa and India, who died in the Ypres Salient area. Since 1928, the Last Post has been played at the Menin Gate every evening at 8 p.m. – except during the German occupation of Ypres in the Second World War (1940–44).

SOURCE D

The Menin Gate.

In the end, the Young Plan came to nothing. In 1929, the Wall Street Crash occurred in the USA; after this, the Americans could not afford to loan any money to Germany. In 1931, the German economy also crashed and the Allies agreed to suspend reparations payments. When Hitler came to power in 1933, he had no intention of paying reparations.

EXAM-STYLE QUESTION

A01   **A02**

Explain **two** effects on Germany of Stresemann's work to reorganise reparations payments.   **(8 marks)**

> **HINT**
>
> When you explain an effect on something, you need to include information about how the situation changed.

ACTIVITY

1 Copy and complete the table below to compare the terms of the Dawes Plan and the Young Plan.
2 Which plan treated Germany more fairly?

	DAWES PLAN 1924	YOUNG PLAN 1929
Amount of reparations		
Timetable for payments		
Terms and conditions		
Effect on Germany		

2.2 STRESEMANN'S SUCCESSES ABROAD

LEARNING OBJECTIVES

Understand the role of Stresemann in developing relations with other countries

Understand the challenges and successes of Stresemann's work as foreign secretary

Understand the criticism that some Germans made about foreign relations at this time.

KEY TERM

diplomacy the use of negotiations and agreements to reach decisions and resolve differences between countries

Stresemann was determined to strengthen Germany's power and wealth. However, he realised that Germany could not challenge the Treaty of Versailles or fight the Allies on military terms. He therefore used **diplomacy** to improve Germany's position. For example, he improved Germany's relationship with other countries, including Britain and France, by ending passive resistance in the Ruhr in 1923. (See page 16 for more information about passive resistance.)

SOURCE E

From a letter written by Stresemann in 1925.

In my opinion there are three great tasks that confront German foreign policy in the immediate future:

1 The solution of the reparations problems in a way that is tolerable for Germany.

2 The protection of those ten to twelve million Germans who now live under foreign control in foreign lands.

3 The readjustment of our eastern frontiers; the recovery of Danzig, the Polish Corridor, and a correction of the frontier in the Upper Silesia.

THE LOCARNO PACT 1925

SOURCE F

Stresemann signing the Locarno Pact. This agreement was negotiated in Locarno, Switzerland and signed in London in 1925.

EXTEND YOUR KNOWLEDGE

GUSTAV STRESEMANN

Gustav Stresemann was the son of a restaurant owner. He was a lonely boy who loved to study. At university, he wrote a paper on the bottled beer trade, but his career was to be in politics. In 1907, aged 29, Stresemann became the youngest member of the Reichstag. He suffered from poor health and was rejected when he attempted to join the German army during the First World War. His health began to decline in 1927 and he was advised to stop work. However, he insisted on continuing as foreign secretary, and held that office until he died of a stroke in October 1929.

In 1925, Germany signed the Locarno Pact. This was a collection of seven treaties involving Germany, France, Belgium, Italy, Britain, Czechoslovakia and Poland.

- Germany agreed to accept its new western borders, and all the countries involved in the Locarno Pact agreed to avoid military force except in self-defence. This provided important reassurance for France and Germany in particular: they shared a long border and the French had invaded the Ruhr in 1923.

- Germany agreed that Alsace-Lorraine would be French. In return, the French agreed not to occupy the Ruhr again.

- All parties agreed that Germany's eastern borders could be settled by 'peaceful means'. Germany, Poland and Czechoslovakia agreed to settle all disputes peacefully through the League of Nations.

Stresemann said the Locarno Pact was a victory, because it made peace in Europe more likely. He said that Germany was now being treated as an equal to the other European powers, rather than being ordered about by them. Despite these arguments, some nationalist parties and groups in Germany were very resentful. They were unhappy that Stresemann was accepting the terms of the Treaty of Versailles, particularly in relation to Germany's borders.

However, the Locarno Pact did lead to a significant improvement in relations between Germany and other countries. Stresemann was awarded the Nobel Peace Prize in 1926 and the period 1925–29 is sometimes called 'the Locarno Honeymoon'.

SOURCE G

Gustav Stresemann talking after the signing of the Locarno Pact in 1925.

The great majority of the German people stands firm for such a peace as this. Relying on this will to peace, we set our signature to this treaty. It is to introduce a new era of cooperation among the nations. It is to close the seven years that followed the War, by a time of real peace, upheld by the will of responsible and far-seeing statesmen, who have shown us the way to such development, and will be supported by their peoples, who know that only in this fashion can prosperity increase. May later generations have cause to bless this day as the beginning of a new era.

ACTIVITY

Read Source G. What can you learn about the Locarno Pact from this source?

SOURCE H

Public protest in Berlin in 1925. This protest was organised by nationalists against the signing of the Locarno treaty.

ACTIVITY

Match up the following statements to make pairs.

STRESEMANN'S STRATEGY	DRAWBACKS
Use diplomacy to improve relations	Germany was getting stronger but was not strong enough to have any genuine power compared with the Allies
Reorganise reparations payments	The nationalists saw building relationships with former enemies as weakness
Build a stronger Germany	Nationalists wanted Germany to refuse to pay altogether
Increase loyalty to the new Weimar Republic	Germany was vulnerable as it relied on loans from the USA
Build an economic recovery	Support for the regime was still limited

SOURCE I

A German cartoon from 1926, showing the 'mask of peace' worn by the French during the Locarno treaties.

LEAGUE OF NATIONS 1926

The League of Nations was formed at the end of the First World War. This was a new international organisation, which allowed powerful countries to discuss ways of solving the world's problems without using military force. No one wanted a repeat of the horrors of the First World War. The idea for the League of Nations came from the US president, Woodrow Wilson. However, the USA chose not to become involved in European politics after the war had ended, and did not join the league. Germany, like the other defeated nations in the war, was not invited to become a member.

In September 1926, Stresemann persuaded the other great powers to allow Germany to join the League of Nations. This was partly a result of the signing of the Locarno Pact. Germany was given a place on the League of Nations Council – this was significant because the members of this council made the most important decisions.

This was a positive step for moderate political parties who supported Stresemann's **diplomatic** policies and his attempts to improve relations with the other great powers. It also increased many Germans' confidence in the Weimar regime: they could see that their country was once more accepted into the 'international family'. However, some Germans saw the League of Nations as a symbol of the hated Treaty of Versailles. They wanted Germany to have nothing to do with it.

ACTIVITY

Look at Source I.
1 What do you think the cartoonist was trying to say?
2 Do you think the following people would have agreed with the cartoonist?
a Stresemann
b a worker in the Ruhr
c a soldier who fought in the First World War.

KELLOGG-BRIAND PACT 1928

In August 1928, 62 countries including Germany, the USA and France signed the Kellogg–Briand Pact. The aim of this pact was to prevent a future war, by getting countries to promise not to use military force to settle disagreements. The pact was named after the US secretary of state and the French foreign minister who wrote the agreement. The USA was not in the League of Nations and it saw this pact as a way for it to be involved in building peace with other countries.

US President Calvin Coolidge signs the Kellogg-Briand Pact in his office. Secretary of State Frank B. Kellogg is seated to the left of the President. The man sitting on Coolidge's right is Charles Dawes.

This pact showed a clear improvement in Germany's relations with other countries.

- Germany had been excluded from the negotiations that led to the Treaty of Versailles. Now, however, Germany was included among the main powers once again.
- It was clear that the Weimar Republic was now a respected, stable state. It had recovered from its troubled beginning.
- This pact gave the German public more confidence that the moderate political parties could be trusted to make Germany strong again.

Of course, there were still many people in Germany who did not approve, because the Kellogg–Briand Pact did nothing to end the hated Treaty of Versailles.

An account of Stresemann's achievements, published in a German newspaper after his death in October 1929.

To serve Germany he set out a path of understanding. He refused to try to get back land that had gone forever. He offered our former enemies friendship. Being a practical man he saw that any other path would have left Germany without any hope of recovery.

EXTRACT A

From a history textbook for schools, published in 2015.

As the economy improved, so social conditions stabilised and political violence died down. Between 1924 and 1929, no major political figures were assassinated. The Weimar government had been in power for long enough for many people to accept that it was now the political system in Germany – as long as things continued to improve. Support for extremist parties (both left wing and right wing) reduced... Coalition governments were still the norm, although they changed less often: between 1924 and 1929, there were just six different coalitions. Stresemann's influence was vital to this. However, none of the weaknesses of the constitution had been resolved. And in 1929, Stresemann died.

ACTIVITY

Study Source K and Extract A.

1 How far do you agree with what the German newspaper said in Source K?
2 What impression does Extract A give of Stresemann's impact on politics in Germany?
3 Hold a class debate about whether you agree with this statement: 'Gustav Stresemann solved the problems of the Weimar Republic'. One half of the class should agree with the statement and the other half should disagree with it.
4 Copy and complete the table below to show how Stresemann's foreign policy helped Germany.

▼ EVENT	▼ IMPACT ON GERMANY
Signing the Locarno Pact	
Joining the League of Nations	
Signing the Kellogg–Briand Pact	

EXAM-STYLE QUESTION

A01   **A02**

SKILLS   PROBLEM SOLVING, REASONING, DECISION MAKING, ADAPTIVE LEARNING, INNOVATION

'The foreign policy of Stresemann was the main reason why Germany recovered in the 1920s.'

How far do you agree? Explain your answer.

You may use the following in your answer:
- the foreign policy of Stresemann
- the Dawes Plan 1924.

You **must** also use information of your own.   **(16 marks)**

HINT

Remember to think about all the reasons why Germany recovered from the problems it faced in the early 1920s. Then explain why at least three of them brought about recovery.

RECAP

RECALL QUIZ

1 What name was given to the 1923 government led by Stresemann?
2 For how many months did Stresemann hold the position of chancellor?
3 What was the name of the new German currency introduced in November 1923?
4 What was the Reichsbank?
5 Under the terms of the Dawes Plan, how much money was lent to Germany by the USA?
6 Which period is sometimes known as the 'Locarno Honeymoon'?
7 What was the League of Nations?
8 Who was Briand?
9 In 1928, how many countries signed the Kellogg–Briand Pact?
10 In which year did Stresemann die?

CHECKPOINT

STRENGTHEN
S1 Describe the measures taken by Stresemann to stabilise the German currency.
S2 Summarise the terms of the Locarno Treaty.
S3 List three points included in the Kellogg–Briand Pact.

CHALLENGE
C1 Why did Stresemann argue that Germany needed to accept the Treaty of Versailles?
C2 Explain the key differences between the Dawes Plan and the Young Plan.
C3 What do you think people meant when they described the years 1925–29 as the 'Locarno Honeymoon'?

SUMMARY

- The period 1923–29 is sometimes called the 'Stresemann Era' because Stresemann played such an important part in German politics at this time.
- Stresemann's economic and diplomatic policies meant that Germany recovered to a large extent from the crisis of 1923.
- Stresemann focused on improving Germany's relations with other countries.
- Stresemann believed that Germany needed to restore good relations with other countries before it could address its economic problems.
- Stresemann took a more moderate approach to German politics. He aimed to reduce the threat of political extremism and build a new, stronger Germany.
- Public confidence in the moderate political parties increased. The German public began to believe that these parties could rebuild Germany's future.
- There were still hardliners in Germany who did not want the Weimar democracy to succeed. They believed that Stresemann's approach involved unacceptable compromises, such as accepting the Treaty of Versailles.

EXAM GUIDANCE: PART (B) QUESTIONS

A01   **A02**

Question to be answered: Explain **two** effects on Germany of the work of Stresemann.
(8 marks)

1 **Analysis Question 1: What is the question type testing?**
In this question, you have to show that you have knowledge and understanding of the key features and characteristics of the period studied.

You also have to analyse historical events and periods so you can explain and make judgements about their effects. In this case, you need to demonstrate your knowledge and understanding of the ways in which Stresemann's work affected Germany.

2 **Analysis Question 2: What do I have to do to answer the question well?**
Obviously, you have to write about Stresemann's work but don't simply write everything you know. You have to write about two effects – things that Stresemann's work caused to happen. The key to explaining the effects of an event is to explain the links between the event and an outcome. For example, an effect of you doing a lot of revision should be that you can answer the questions in the exam more effectively. You would explain this by emphasising that you know more facts, you have to spend less time trying to remember things, you have looked at more examples of how to answer questions, and so on.

3 **Analysis Question 3: Are there any techniques I can use to make it very clear that I am doing what is needed to be successful?**
This is an 8-mark question and you need to make sure you leave enough time to answer the other two questions fully (they are worth 22 marks in total). Remember, you do not need to write an essay – you simply need to identify two effects and provide enough historical detail to explain why the event had these effects.

The question asks for two effects, so it's a good idea to write two paragraphs and to begin each paragraph with a phrase such as: 'One effect was…', 'Another effect was…'. You should also try to use phrases such as: 'this led to…'; 'as a result of this…'; 'this brought about…'. This will help to show that you are focusing on effects.

The word 'explain' is important because it tells you that you have to do more than just state what the effect was. You need to use your knowledge of the period to explain how the event (Stresemann's work) led to the outcome. So 'this led to…' is simply stating an effect, but 'this led to… because at this time…' is moving towards an explanation.

You cannot get more than 4 marks if you explain only one effect. However, you are required to explain only two effects and you will not gain credit for a third. If you do write about more than two effects, the better two will be marked and the third will be ignored.

Answer A

In 1923 the hyperinflation crisis meant money in Germany became worthless. Stresemann brought in a new currency to fix the problem. His actions helped Germany a lot.

What are the strengths and weaknesses of Answer A?

This is a very weak answer. It identifies one of Stresemann's actions (introducing a new currency) and states that this helped to deal with hyperinflation, but it does not provide sufficient detail. The answer does not explain how Stresemann's actions helped Germany or why the new currency helped to solve the hyperinflation crisis and restore confidence. The answer needs much more detail to score a high mark.

Answer B

One effect of Stresemann's work was that he stabilised the German economy and ended the crisis which was making it so difficult to govern effectively. Hyperinflation had gripped Germany in 1923, but Stresemann's measure to introduce a new temporary currency – the Rentenmark – and link its value to Germany's industrial and agricultural worth restored business and public confidence in the German currency. The new independent Reichsbank was given control of Germany's currency in 1924 which gave longer term stability.

Another feature of Stresemann's work was that Germany's relations with other countries improved dramatically and it rejoined the 'family of nations'. Stresemann was convinced that foreign affairs could benefit Germany at home because improving the terms of reparations payments, for example, could help the German economy. Stresemann successfully negotiated the Locarno Treaties and was responsible for Germany joining the League of Nations in 1926. This meant that Germany was once again seen as a leading power and was more accepted internationally after the shame and humiliation of losing the First World War and the 'diktat' of the Treaty of Versailles.

What are the strengths and weaknesses of Answer B?

This is a very good answer. Two important effects of Stresemann's work – economic effects and improved international relations – are discussed and good details are provided to support the explanation. The events in the Ruhr would have been a very useful alternative factor, as it affected both economic and foreign relations issues.

Challenge a friend

Use the Student Book to set a part (b) question for a friend. Then look at the answer. Does it do the following things?

☐ Identify two effects

☐ Provide 3–4 lines of detailed historical knowledge to explain why the event caused each outcome (effect) you have identified.

If it does, you can tell your friend that the answer is very good!

3. THE RISE OF HITLER AND THE NAZIS TO JANUARY 1933

LEARNING OBJECTIVES

- ☐ Understand the origins and growth of the Nazi Party
- ☐ Understand the impact of the Great Depression on Nazi support
- ☐ Understand how the events of 1932 led to Hitler becoming chancellor.

The Nazi Party was formed in Munich after the end of the First World War and was, at first, a fairly insignificant political group. This chapter will help you to understand how the Nazi Party developed between 1919 and 1933. From the mid-1920s, the Nazi Party changed its organisation and began to use new tactics to try to gain power. By the late 1920s, the Nazis were in a position to take advantage of the unstable economic situation in Germany. When the Weimar democracy collapsed, due to the Great Depression, Hitler presented himself as the leader Germany needed to become strong again. In 1933, Hitler became chancellor of Germany and the Nazi Party took power.

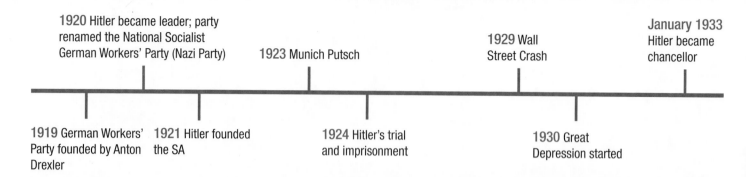

1920 Hitler became leader; party renamed the National Socialist German Workers' Party (Nazi Party)

1923 Munich Putsch

1929 Wall Street Crash

January 1933 Hitler became chancellor

1919 German Workers' Party founded by Anton Drexler

1921 Hitler founded the SA

1924 Hitler's trial and imprisonment

1930 Great Depression started

3.1 HITLER AND THE GERMAN WORKERS' PARTY 1920–22

LEARNING OBJECTIVES

- Understand the origins of Hitler's political ideas
- Understand the beginnings of the German Workers' Party and changes 1920–22
- Understand the aims and features of the Nazi Party.

THE ORIGINS OF THE NAZI PARTY

When the First World War started in 1914, Hitler was living in Munich, Bavaria. He joined the army in 1914 and served as a soldier on the Western Front in France. The conditions were terrible and many of the men he fought with were killed. By the end of the first week, only 611 men from his regiment of 3,600 had survived. During the war, Hitler was promoted to corporal and awarded the Iron Cross medal for bravery. Like many other soldiers, he could not believe the news when he heard that Germany had lost the war: their superiors had assured them of victory and they had believed that their sacrifices would pay off.

After the war ended, many Germans felt betrayed. They did not trust the government and wanted new ideas about how to rebuild Germany. As a result, many extreme political groups gained support after the war. From 1919, Hitler worked for the army to monitor the activities of these groups in Germany. One of the groups Hitler was spying on was the German Workers' Party, which had been formed in January 1919 and was led by Anton Drexler. Although the party had only six members at that time, Hitler attended the party meetings to gather information. Over time, he came to realise that he agreed with the views of the party. It believed:

1 democracy was weak and a powerful leader was needed to rebuild Germany's strength
2 Jews were to blame for making Germany weak
3 Communists and Socialists had brought about the fall of the Kaiser
4 the socialist Weimar politicians had betrayed Germany by signing the Treaty of Versailles.

Hitler joined the German Workers' Party in September 1919. At the time, the party seemed very unimportant but it rapidly became more popular over the next few years.

SOURCE A

From a confidential Interior Ministry report on the Nazi Party in the 1920s.

In spite of their very well prepared and thoroughly organised propaganda, their successes remain very minor. This party isn't going anywhere. Today it is a splinter group that can't exert any real influence on the great mass of the population.

ACTIVITY

1 What impression does the author of Source A give about the impact of the Nazi Party on Germany in the 1920s?
2 Why did the Interior Ministry collect information on political parties like the Nazi Party?

EXTEND YOUR KNOWLEDGE

HITLER THE ARTIST

Hitler was born in a small town in Austria in 1889. He did badly at school where his favourite subject was art. After he finished school, he went to live in Vienna where he hoped to become an artist. Unfortunately, he was rejected by both the Vienna Academy of Art and the School of Architecture. With little money, he stayed at a hostel and painted postcards which he hoped to sell. Some people claim that Hitler developed a hatred for Jews at this time, because he was convinced that a Jewish professor had rejected his art work. He also blamed a Jewish doctor for his mother's death.

CHANGES TO THE PARTY, 1920–22

KEY TERM

propaganda information (sometimes misleading) that is used to persuade people to hold or believe in certain values and ideas

In February 1920, Hitler was put in charge of **propaganda** for the German Workers' Party. In this role, he played an important part in increasing party membership. In the same year:

- Hitler and Drexler rewrote the aims of the party; the revised aims were published in its 25 Point Programme
- the party was renamed the National Socialist German Workers' Party (NSDAP) or the Nazi Party.

By 1921, Hitler had become the party leader. The party's aims were kept deliberately vague, so they would appeal to many different groups in Germany. For example:

- nationalists were keen on the destruction of the Treaty of Versailles
- people who wanted someone to blame for Germany's problems and defeat in the First World War were attracted by the party's **anti-Semitism**
- the middle classes and big businesses liked Hitler's anti-communist ideas.

SOURCE B

Key points from the German Workers' Party 25 Point Programme, 1920.

We demand the union of all Germans in a greater Germany on the basis of national self-determination.

We demand the revocation (end) of the peace treaties of Versailles and Saint Germain.

We demand land and territory to feed our people and settle our extra population.

Only those of German blood may be members of the nation.

ACTIVITY

1 Describe the aims of the German Workers' Party.
2 What do these demands suggest about Hitler's beliefs about race?

HITLER'S ROLE 1920–22

Hitler was a talented speaker and attracted many new members to the Nazi Party. He argued that Germany needed a strong authoritarian government and this message was popular among critics of the Weimar Republic. Hitler's leadership and the role of other new members, including Ernst Röhm, meant that the party was no longer one that could be ignored. By the end of 1920 membership had increased to around 1,100 and as a result the party could afford to purchase a newspaper which it called the *People's Observer*. Hitler was now the undisputed leader of the party (see Figure 3.1) and decided it was time to have a military wing in the party to help promote its views.

Talented speaker

Appealed to critics of the Weimar Republic

Controlled the NSDAP like a military leader

Suggested the name change that was made in August 1920

Introduced the emblem of the swastika, and the arm salute

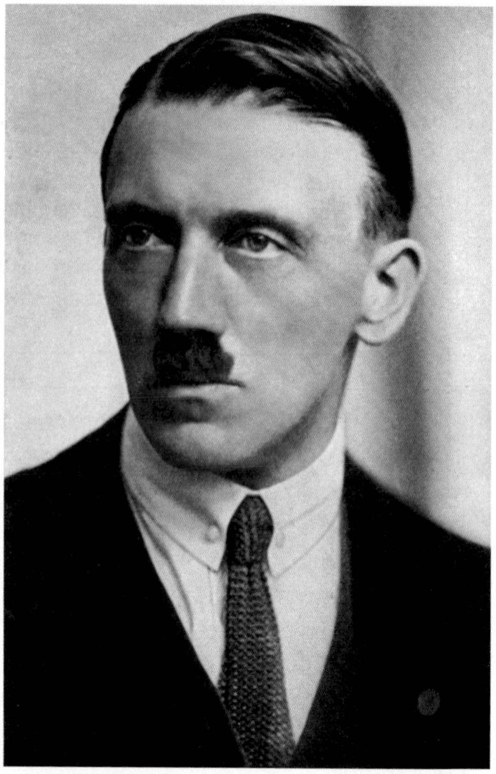

Ousted Drexler and became leader in mid-1921

Used the party newspaper (*Völkischer Beobachter*) to spread the party's views

Surrounded himself with loyal individuals such as Röhm, Goering and Hess

Developed friendships with powerful Germans such as General Ludendorff (the German army commander in the First World War)

▲ **Figure 3.1** Hitler's role in the growth of the Nazi Party, 1920–22

ACTIVITY

Complete a table with the headings 'Hitler's measures' and 'How this helped the Nazi Party'.

EXTEND YOUR KNOWLEDGE

THE VÖLKISCHER BEOBACHTER – THE PEOPLE'S OBSERVER

The *Völkischer Beobachter* was the first Nazi newspaper, published between 1920 and 1945. It was not originally a Nazi newspaper – it had started as the *Münchener Beobachter* (Munich Observer), which focused on lighter news stories and gossip. After the First World War, however, it became a voice of extreme anti-Semitism. On 10 March 1920, the main headline was 'Clean Out the Jews Once and For All'; the article below called for the German government to sweep out the 'Jewish vermin with an iron broom'. In 1920, the paper had money troubles and was bought by members of the German Workers' Party.

THE ORIGINS OF THE STURMABTEILUNG (SA)

KEY TERM

paramilitary force a private group run like a military force

Many ex-soldiers, such as the Freikorps, were attracted to Hitler's ideas. They shared his sense of nationalism and resented the settlement after the First World War. In 1921, Hitler set up the *Sturmabteilung* (SA), sometimes called the **stormtroopers**. Ernst Röhm, one of Hitler's loyal supporters at the time, became the leader of the SA. The SA wore brown shirts as a uniform, so they were sometimes called the 'Brownshirts'. Members of the SA were provided with uniforms, meals and hostel accommodation. The SA was created as a **paramilitary force**; their role was to disrupt the meetings of opposing political parties and control crowds at Nazi meetings. There was often violence between Communists and SA members.

The power and organisation of the SA impressed many people. The SA paraded in the streets as a show of force and to demonstrate Hitler's strength. Many SA members were unruly characters who could be difficult to control. However, Hitler demanded their complete obedience to him (even though Ernst Röhm was the official head of the SA). Hitler chose the most-trusted members of the SA to be his own personal **bodyguard**, known as the *Stosstrupp* (Shock Troop).

3.2 THE MUNICH PUTSCH AND THE REORGANISATION OF THE NAZI PARTY

LEARNING OUTCOMES

- Understand the causes and events of the Munich Putsch
- Understand the results of the Munich Putsch
- Understand how the Nazi Party was reorganised in the period 1924–28

CAUSES OF THE MUNICH PUTSCH

In November 1923, Hitler led an armed uprising known as the Munich Putsch or the Beer Hall Putsch. The intention was to overthrow the Weimar Republic. What made Hitler carry out such a bold move?

- From 1918 to 1923, many Germans had developed a deep anger towards the Weimar Republic. They were angry about issues such as the 'stab in the back', reparations and the loss of Germany's colonies. As a result, support for nationalist parties like NSDAP had grown significantly in Bavaria.

- The leaders of the Bavarian state government, including Gustav von Kahr, were hostile to the Weimar government. They agreed with the NSDAP's views and sometimes chose to ignore SA violence. Hitler knew he would have support in Munich.

- During 1923, Germany's economic position had worsened. In 1923, French troops marched into the Ruhr (the German industrial heartland) and took over German businesses there. Germans who resisted were imprisoned or even **deported**. The Weimar Republic seemed unable to resolve the situation and many German people saw the government as weak and powerless. As hyperinflation reached its peak in November 1923, Hitler saw an opportunity to take power.

- From 1921 to 1922, Hitler and the Nazis were influenced by the Fascists, an Italian right-wing party led by Benito Mussolini. The Nazis copied the Fascists' **salute** and use of flags and this helped to give the Nazi Party a clear identity. In 1922, Mussolini led his paramilitary soldiers in a 'march on Rome'. He used violence to force the Italian democratic government to accept him as leader of Italy. Hitler decided to use a similar approach in Germany to take power for himself.

- Hitler believed the Nazi Party was ready to seize power. It had 20,000 supporters and the SA, its own private army. Hitler had built a close relationship with the former army leader, General Ludendorff. Hitler believed Ludendorff could persuade the army to support the Nazi Party against the Weimar government; this would make a **takeover** possible.

▽ MEMBERSHIP OF THE NAZI PARTY 1920–28	
1920	1,100
1923	20,000
1925	27,000
1928	108,000

SOURCE C

Members of the SA boarding a lorry just before the attempted putsch.

WHO'S WHO IN THE MUNICH PUTSCH?

The key characters involved in the Munich Putsch are shown in Figure 3.2.

Otto von Lossow

■ Head of the German army in Bavaria

■ Fled during the Putsch to join the opposition to Hitler

Gustav von Kahr

■ Bavarian prime minister

■ Supported Hitler's aims

Erich Ludendorff

■ With Hitler, sought Kahr's support in the Putsch

■ Led the Putsch along with Hitler and was arrested as a result

▲ **Figure 3.2** Who's who in the Munich Putsch?

EXAM-STYLE QUESTION

AO4

SKILLS ANALYSIS, INTERPRETATION, CREATIVITY

Study Extract A.

What impression does the author of Extract A give about Hitler's leadership of the Munich Putsch?

You **must** use Extract A to explain your answer. **(6 marks)**

HINT

Think about the author's criticisms of Hitler's leadership qualities. Then explain what he says about the other people involved in the Munich Putsch.

A historian commenting on the Munich Putsch in a book written in 1992.

Hitler… proved singularly ineffective. Nothing had been properly planned… He remained shut up in the Beer Hall… unable to make up his mind whether or not to risk a demonstration. It was Ludendorff who decided for him, and at noon the next day led out Hitler and the other Nazi leaders at the head of a column of several thousand men, which… marched into the centre of the city. While Ludendorff marched on and pushed through the [police] cordon, Hitler, after being pulled to the ground and dislocating his arm, scrambled to his feet and fled.

WHAT HAPPENED IN THE MUNICH PUTSCH?

The main events of the Munich Putsch are shown in Figure 3.3.

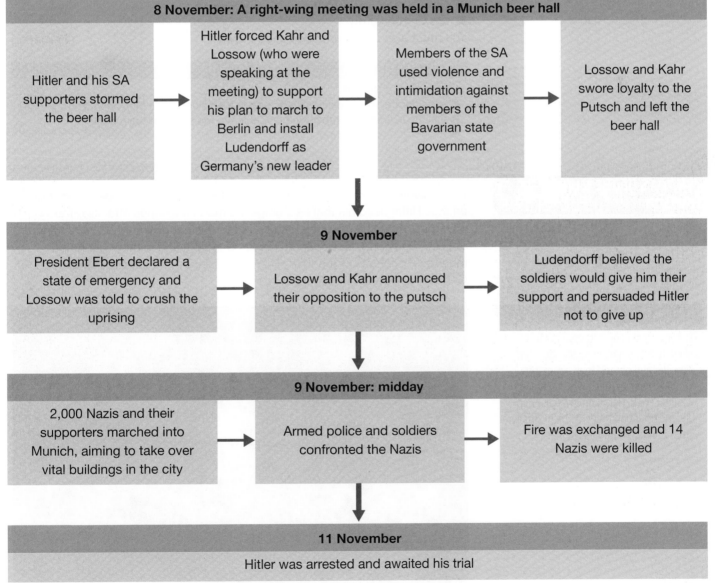

8 November: A right-wing meeting was held in a Munich beer hall

Hitler and his SA supporters stormed the beer hall → Hitler forced Kahr and Lossow (who were speaking at the meeting) to support his plan to march to Berlin and install Ludendorff as Germany's new leader → Members of the SA used violence and intimidation against members of the Bavarian state government → Lossow and Kahr swore loyalty to the Putsch and left the beer hall

9 November

President Ebert declared a state of emergency and Lossow was told to crush the uprising → Lossow and Kahr announced their opposition to the putsch → Ludendorff believed the soldiers would give him their support and persuaded Hitler not to give up

9 November: midday

2,000 Nazis and their supporters marched into Munich, aiming to take over vital buildings in the city → Armed police and soldiers confronted the Nazis → Fire was exchanged and 14 Nazis were killed

11 November

Hitler was arrested and awaited his trial

▲ **Figure 3.3** The main events of the Munich Putsch

ACTIVITY

1 Work in small groups to create a series of 'living photographs' by acting out key moments during the Munich Putsch. Use Figure 3.3 to help you identify the key events.

2 Perform a selection of your living photographs to the other students and ask them to identify the events you are showing.

EXAM-STYLE QUESTION

A01   **A02**

SKILLS PROBLEM SOLVING, REASONING, DECISION MAKING, ADAPTIVE LEARNING, INNOVATION

'The most important reason for the failure of the Munich Putsch was Hitler's poor leadership.'

How far do you agree? Explain your answer.

You may use the following in your answer:
■ Hitler's poor leadership
■ the German army.
You **must** also use information of your own.   **(16 marks)**

HINT

A good answer should:
■ consider the role of Hitler's leadership in the failure of the Munich Putsch
■ include a number of other factors that led to the failure of the putsch
■ make a judgement about how far Hitler's leadership was the reason for the failure of the Munich Putsch.

RESULTS OF THE MUNICH PUTSCH

In February 1924, Hitler, Ludendorff, Röhm and other Nazi leaders were put on trial. Hitler used his trial as a stage: he made speeches attacking the government and claimed the leaders of the Weimar government were traitors, not him (Source E). Newspapers across Germany and in other countries reported the events of the trial. Hitler was seen as a nationalist standing up for German rights and his popularity grew.

SOURCE D

The principal people involved in the Munich Putsch pose outside the court after the end of their trial. (From left to right: Heinz Pernet, Friedrich Weber, Wilhelm Frick, Hermann Kriebel, Erich Ludendorff, Adolf Hitler, Wilhelm Brückner, Ernst Röhm and Robert Wagner).

SOURCE E

Hitler speaks at his trial in 1924.

I alone bear the responsibility. But I am not a criminal because of that. If today I stand here as a revolutionary, it is as a revolutionary against the revolution. There is no such thing as high treason against the traitors of 1918.

There was no doubt that Hitler would be found guilty, but his speeches seemed to have impressed the judges. Hitler and three others were found guilty of **treason** and he was sentenced to 5 years in jail at Landsberg Castle. This was a very light sentence given the serious nature of the crimes. Conditions in the jail were very relaxed, and Hitler enjoyed a number of home comforts. He also won an early release so, in the end, he spent only 9 months in jail. Ludendorff was found not guilty – mainly because of the judge's sympathy for the great war hero. (There was plenty of evidence against him.) However, the Nazi Party was banned.

It looked as though the Munich Putsch had achieved little – except to have the Nazi Party banned and its leaders imprisoned. However, there were successes. The judge could have ordered the **execution** of Hitler and the other leaders but instead, he gave them a very light sentence. This showed that there were still powerful forces in Germany who wanted the Weimar government destroyed. Hitler's imprisonment gave him the opportunity to write his book, *Mein Kampf* (My Struggle), in which he outlined his beliefs. Rudolf Hess, who later became deputy leader of the Nazis, was in prison with Hitler; Hitler dictated his ideas and Hess wrote them down.

SOURCE F

Hitler speaking in 1933 about the failure of the Munich Putsch.

The sudden takeover of power in the whole of Germany would have led to the greatest difficulties as the preparations had not begun by the National Socialist Party. The events of 1923 with their blood sacrifice have proved the most effective propaganda.

ACTIVITY

Read sources E and F.
1 In what ways did Hitler use the trial to promote his ideas?
2 Why did Hitler consider the Nazi Party was not ready for power in 1923?
3 Is it fair to describe the Munich Putsch as a complete failure?

THE REORGANISATION OF THE NAZI PARTY 1924–28

KEY TERMS

Lebensraum 'living room'; areas of land that the Nazis claimed they would need to acquire to provide space for a growing Aryan population

Aryans those people who Hitler said were the master race

The ban on the Nazi Party was lifted in February 1925 and Hitler decided to relaunch the party. He chose to make his return in the same Munich Beer Hall that had been the location of the Munich Putsch. The rally was attended by 4,000 supporters. Hitler's book, *Mein Kampf*, was published in the same year and soon became a bestseller. It contained many of the key beliefs which Hitler would put into practice from 1933, including: measures against the Jews; the need for more living space (*Lebensraum*) for Germans; and the dominance of the **Aryan** race (see Figure 3.4).

▶ **Figure 3.4** Key ideas in *Mein Kampf*

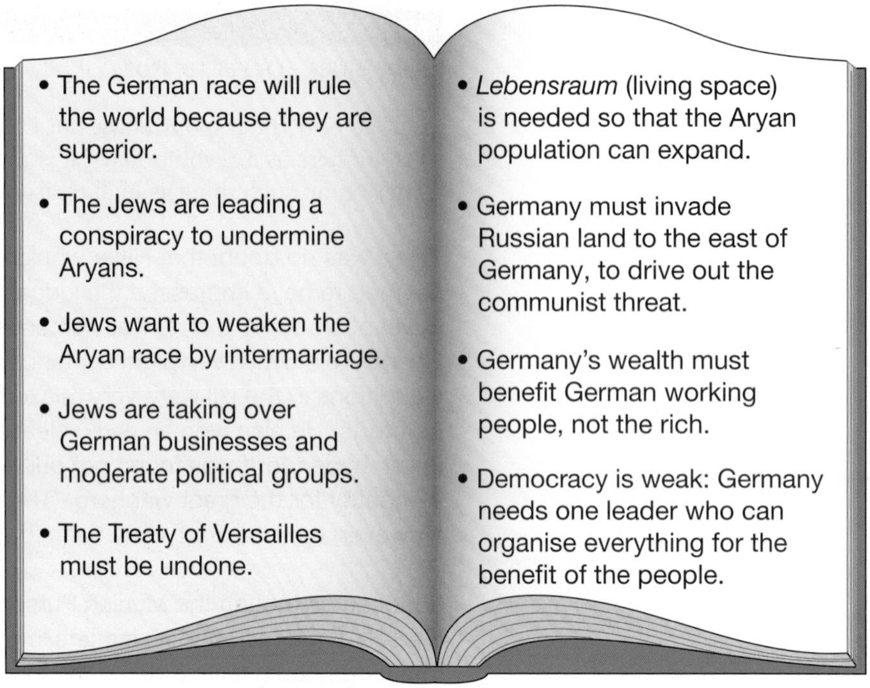

- The German race will rule the world because they are superior.

- The Jews are leading a conspiracy to undermine Aryans.

- Jews want to weaken the Aryan race by intermarriage.

- Jews are taking over German businesses and moderate political groups.

- The Treaty of Versailles must be undone.

- *Lebensraum* (living space) is needed so that the Aryan population can expand.

- Germany must invade Russian land to the east of Germany, to drive out the communist threat.

- Germany's wealth must benefit German working people, not the rich.

- Democracy is weak: Germany needs one leader who can organise everything for the benefit of the people.

While in prison, Hitler had become convinced that the Nazi Party needed to change its methods. They had failed to take power by violent revolution; instead, they should try to win support by legal means (Source G). With this in mind, Hitler began to reorganise the party to make it more attractive to German voters.

- He created a national headquarters for the Nazi Party in Munich.
- He divided Germany into 34 districts, and appointed a leading Nazi to increase support in each district.
- In 1926, he called a party conference in Bamberg. Here, he was confirmed as leader. At the conference, he persuaded party members to re-adopt the 25 Point Plan.
- In 1926, the first Nazi rally was held in Weimar.
- Hitler encouraged more young people to join the SA and also set up the Hitler Youth.
- Hitler established a new private bodyguard called the *Schutzstaffel* (SS).
- Goebbels, who edited the Nazi newspaper and was in charge of propaganda, emphasised the Nazi's opposition to Jews. This anti-Jewish message was very popular.
- The Nazis held public meetings across Germany and trained their members to be effective public speakers.
- The Nazi Party established various organisations, such as the Nazi Women's League, to take its message to particular groups of people.
- The party concentrated on winning the support of farmers, as Germany's agriculture was suffering badly in the late 1920s.

ACTIVITY

What do you think Hitler meant in Source G when he said the Nazis would 'have to hold our noses'?

SOURCE G

Hitler speaking in the mid-1920s.

Instead of working to achieve power by armed coup, we shall have to hold our noses and enter the Reichstag against the opposition deputies. If outvoting them takes longer than outshooting them, at least the results will be guaranteed by their own constitution.

SOURCE H

An American journalist remembering the support he saw for the Nazis in 1928.

Support for the Nazi Party had grown due to the country's problems of hyperinflation and the French invasion of the Ruhr. By 1928 Nazism appeared to be a dying cause. Now that Germany's outlook was suddenly bright, the Nazi Party was rapidly withering away. One scarcely heard of Hitler or the Nazis except as a joke.

SOURCE I

Hitler speaks to supporters in 1925.

LIMITED SUPPORT FOR THE NAZIS, 1923–29

By 1929 – thanks to Hitler's reorganisation – the Nazi party was well organised, with a membership of over 100,000. However, the Nazis had little success in gaining seats in the Reichstag. In May 1924 (in which the Nazis stood as the National Socialist Freedom Movement because the NSDAP was banned following the Munich Putsch) they won 32 seats. Four years later, in 1928, they managed to win only 12 seats.

This was largely because of Gustav Stresemann's efforts. Between 1924 and 1929, Stresemann had ended inflation and agreed the Dawes and Young Plans. This had helped to stabilise the German economy. As foreign minister, Stresemann had restored Germany's place in the international community: the Locarno and Kellogg–Briand Pacts had improved Germany's relations with other countries and, in 1926, Germany had become part of the League of Nations. In 1925, Hindenburg had become president of the Republic. He had been an army commander in the First World War and was popular among Germans with more **conservative** and nationalist views. He and Stresemann managed to unite the more moderate parties on both the left and the right, so coalitions had been able to govern Germany effectively.

As a result, the German people were happier with the government and had less reason to vote for extreme parties, such as the Nazis. In 1928, the Nazis had support from the farming community, winning up to 18 per cent of the vote in some farming areas. The party won few votes in the big cities and industrial areas, however, gaining only 1 per cent of the votes in Berlin and in the Ruhr industrial region.

3.3 IMPACT OF THE GREAT DEPRESSION

LEARNING OBJECTIVES

Understand the economic impact of the Great Depression

Understand the impact of this on support for the Nazi Party

Understand Nazi methods to win support during the Great Depression

In October 1929, Stresemann died suddenly after a stroke. This was a serious setback for the Weimar Republic. At the same time, events in the USA plunged the world economy into a crisis. In Germany, these events gave Hitler the ideal opportunity to gain more support.

THE WALL STREET CRASH, 1929

During the 1920s there had been a great deal of **speculation** on the New York stock exchange (Wall Street) and prices of stocks and shares rose. Then in October 1929, there was a collapse of prices as investors lost confidence and began to sell. As a result, many American businesses were destroyed by the Wall Street Crash. This, in turn, triggered a downturn in the US economy.

The USA recalled the loans it had made to Germany. This led to a financial crisis in Germany, because the government did not have the money to repay the loans. Many German businesses were forced to close due to the economic problems, so many people lost their jobs. Unemployment increased rapidly and the government needed more money to pay unemployment benefits; it raised taxes to provide this money.

THE EFFECTS OF THE GREAT DEPRESSION ON THE GERMAN PEOPLE

Different groups of people were affected in different ways by the Great Depression. The Great Depression led to a spiral of decline and widespread hardship and suffering across many groups in German society. Thousands of German businesses were forced to close and millions lost their jobs as a result. The government took the decision to cut unemployment benefits which meant further suffering and a decline in demand for manufactured products.

- **Young people:** In 1933, more than 50 per cent of people aged 16–30 were unemployed. Even people with a good level of education (such as a university degree) could not find work.
- **Factory workers:** Four out of ten could not get a job. They also suffered because unemployment benefits were reduced by the government. Food prices were high and many unemployed people could not afford to eat.
- **Farmers:** Since the mid-1920s, farmers had been struggling because the price of their goods was falling. Many farmers were in debt. The economic problems in rural areas led to an increase in support for the Nazis. The Nazis used existing farmers' organisations to spread their influence and take advantage of the economic troubles that farmers faced, like falling prices for their goods.
- **Businessmen:** Those who managed to keep their businesses struggled, because people had less money to spend on goods. This was partly because many people were unemployed and partly because of the government tax rises.

People queuing at a job centre in Germany, 1930.

Figure 3.5 shows how unemployment levels in Germany rose and fell between 1928 and 1933.

▶ **Figure 3.5** The growth of unemployment 1928–33

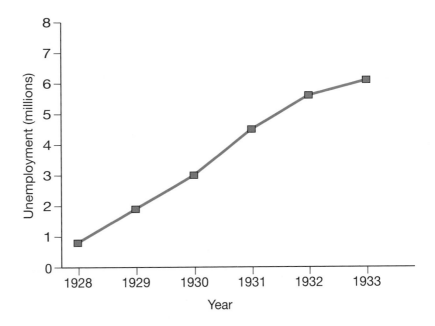

THE EFFECTS OF THE GREAT DEPRESSION ON THE WEIMAR REPUBLIC

As a result of the Great Depression, the SDP and the Centre Party (the two main parties in the coalition government) fell out. Heinrich Brüning (the Centre Party leader) suggested making further cuts to welfare benefits, but Hermann Müller (the SDP leader) refused to accept this. Müller resigned and Brüning became chancellor.

KEY TERMS

Article 48 part of the German constitution; in an emergency, the president could make laws by decree, without the approval of the Reichstag

scapegoats people who are blamed for something that someone else has done wrong

Brüning did not have a majority in the Reichstag, so he asked President Hindenburg to use **Article 48** of the constitution. This could be used in an emergency, so that laws could be made without Reichstag approval. This meant that, from 1930, Germany was not run as a democracy. The Reichstag met only occasionally and Germany was effectively controlled by Hindenburg.

Brüning introduced several unpopular measures, including tax rises and further cuts to unemployment benefit. These measures greatly increased the suffering of the German people. In response, many Germans turned to extreme political parties, in the hopes of a solution to their problems. The Nazis gave people **scapegoats**; they claimed that Germany's problems had been caused by Jews, Communists and Weimar politicians. In the 1930 election, the Nazis won 107 seats and the Communists won 77 seats.

ACTIVITY

1 What was the Wall Street Crash?
2 Describe how the economic depression affected groups in Germany in different ways.
3 Explain the link between the Wall Street Crash and the economic depression in Germany.

EXTRACT A

A modern historian describes the effects of Brüning's policies as chancellor.

He deliberately deepened the economic crisis as he hoped it would allow Germany to recover more quickly… He broke the spirit of the constitution. This contributed to the final destruction of the Weimar Republic and produced an atmosphere of hopelessness.

EXAM-STYLE QUESTION

A01 **A02**

SKILLS PROBLEM SOLVING, REASONING, DECISION MAKING, ADAPTIVE LEARNING, INNOVATION

'The Wall Street Crash was to blame for the economic and social problems in Germany 1929–32.'

How far do you agree? Explain your answer.

You may use the following in your answer:
- the Wall Street Crash
- Brüning's policies.

You **must** also use information of your own.

(16 marks)

HINT

Remember to consider:
- the effects of the Wall Street Crash and the fact that Germany was affected more than some other countries
- other reasons for Germany's economic and social problems
- the difficulties faced by the Weimar government as they tried to provide solutions to these problems.

You need to reach a conclusion about the most important causes.

WHY WAS HITLER ABLE TO BECOME CHANCELLOR?

The Nazis used a number of methods to take advantage of the economic and political problems of the Weimar Republic. They focused on:

- the appeal of Hitler
- the activities of the SA
- skilful use of propaganda.

▼ Seats won by the German Communist Party in elections to the Reichstag

ELECTION	NO OF SEATS	% OF VOTE
1928	54	10.6
1930	77	13.1
1932 (July)	89	14.6
1932 (Nov)	100	16.9

THE APPEAL OF HITLER

During election campaigns in 1930–32, the Nazis presented Hitler as the strong leader that Germany needed and was looking for. In posters, his appearance was changed and he was shown to have almost superhuman strength. When making speeches, for example at Nazi rallies, Hitler developed a powerful and convincing personal style. He said he was Germany's last hope and he promised a better future. These messages were very popular with people who were desperate to see Germany become strong again. Hitler made sure his messages would appeal to many different groups in Germany, with broad pledges such as 'Make Germany strong' and 'Smash the chains of Versailles'.

Powerful business interests were willing to support Hitler and provide financial backing for his campaign with the aim of stopping the rise of communist support. The Communists told the German people that the depression in Germany and worldwide was clear evidence that the capitalist system did not work. They also pointed out that it was the workers who suffered the consequences of this failure when they lost their jobs and couldn't support their families. It was time for the German people to stand up to big business and bring about a fairer society. It was no surprise that the major German business leaders looked for a party that could stop the growth in support for the German Communist Party (see Table).

After 1929 the National Party which had previously attracted the support of big business in Germany had been in decline, so industrialists began to favour Hitler as an alternative. Some wealthy business owners like Krupps and Siemens gave money to help the Nazis promote their message.

SOURCE K

Marching members of the SA, 1930.

THE ROLE OF THE SA

In the SA, the Nazis had a stronger private army than their main rivals – the Communists. The SA played a key role in the growth of the Nazi Party at this time.

- In 1930, the SA had 400,000 members, and their presence at Nazi Party rallies helped the Nazis to appear strong.
- At rallies, the SA used lights and symbols of power such as swords and flags. These reinforced the idea that the Nazis could bring a better future for Germans.
- The SA disrupted the meetings of political opponents.
- In the elections of 1930 and 1932, the SA used violence to threaten the opposition. Some people were killed and voters were intimidated as they cast their votes at polling stations.

EXTEND YOUR KNOWLEDGE

HITLER OVER GERMANY

Many of Goebbels' techniques were very modern for the time. The use of mass media to gain political popularity was only just beginning. Goebbels organised an impressive election schedule: Hitler was flown all over Germany in his *Deutschlandflug* (flight over Germany), using the slogan 'The Führer over Germany'. At one point, Hitler spoke at major rallies in twenty different cities in just 6 days.

NAZI ELECTION PROPAGANDA

The Nazi Party trained members of local groups in propaganda skills. It focused on popular messages and was quick to change its messages if a particular idea began to lose support. For example, at one point, the Nazis were keen to nationalise industry. However, this message was quickly dropped when it became apparent that German industrialists did not support the idea.

The Nazis were keen to use new technology, so Hitler was flown around Germany to make speeches. Goebbels was also a master of propaganda and used many methods to get Nazi messages across to voters. For example:

- Parades and marches were organised by mobile Nazi units. They included both political speeches and entertainments such as plays, concerts and sport.
- The Nazis owned eight different newspapers. Each paper aimed to sell the Nazi message to a particular audience.
- Huge rallies were held, to demonstrate the order and discipline of the Nazi Party.
- Posters were designed to target different groups in Germany. The messages were deliberately clear and simple.

SOURCE L

A Nazi election poster, 1932. The poster is titled 'We farmers of rubbish' and shows an Aryan farmer with a pitchfork clearing up the 'muck' – Communists, Jews and businessmen who have been destroying Germany.

EXAM-STYLE QUESTION

A01 **A02**

Explain **two** effects on the German people of Hitler's methods to win their support in 1932.

(8 marks)

HINT

Make sure you explain two different effects. For example, you could think about the effects of SA intimidation on how people felt about Nazi power.

1932 ELECTIONS AND THE FALL OF BRÜNING

KEY TERM

decree an official order by an individual or group which has the force of law; Article 48 of the Weimar Constitution allowed the president to pass decrees in times of national emergency

In July 1932, the Nazis were the biggest party in the Reichstag with 230 seats (37.4 per cent of the vote). In the same year, Hitler used the elections for president to increase his political reputation in Germany: in April 1932, he polled 13 million votes. In the end, he was beaten by Hindenburg, who kept his role as president. Despite this defeat, Hitler had become a major political figure.

In the same month, Brüning tried to use a presidential **decree** to ban the SA and the SS, because there had been considerable political unrest. However, an ambitious army general named Kurt von Schleicher removed Brüning and replaced him with a coalition of army officers, rich landowners and industrialists. Von Schleicher then persuaded Hindenburg to sack Brüning as chancellor.

FRANZ VON PAPEN

Von Schleicher was determined to take control. He decided that a wealthy politician named von Papen would make a suitable figurehead for a new coalition. Von Schleicher gave Hitler a place in the coalition but he dramatically underestimated Hitler's ability to manipulate the situation to suit his own ends.

The coalition led by von Papen was weak and Hitler argued that he should be chancellor, since the Nazi Party had the largest number of seats in the Reichstag. Hindenburg refused, because he hated Hitler and thought he was becoming too ambitious. Von Papen called another election; the Nazi position was weakened but they remained the largest party in the Reichstag, with 190 seats. As a result, von Papen resigned.

VON SCHLEICHER AND HINDENBURG

KEY TERM

conspiracy a secret plan with other people to do something bad or illegal

Powerful businessmen in Germany wrote to President Hindenburg, asking him to appoint Hitler as chancellor. Hindenburg refused and chose von Schleicher instead. As chancellor, von Schleicher asked Hindenburg to suspend the constitution and make him the head of a military **dictatorship**; he claimed that Hitler and von Papen were trying to lead a **conspiracy** against him. However, von Schleicher's request was leaked and he lost the support of the Reichstag.

Meanwhile, von Papen had become determined to take power. He believed he would be able to control Hitler from the background, and tried to persuade Hindenburg to make him vice chancellor, with Hitler as chancellor. Eventually, Hindenburg agreed and Hitler became chancellor of Germany on 30 January 1933.

▶ **Figure 3.6** The roles of von Papen, Schleicher and Hindenburg in Hitler becoming chancellor

April 1932: Chancellor Brüning banned the SA and the SS using a presidential decree to calm political unrest. This made the right wing angry. Army General von Schleicher organised a right-wing coalition, including army officers and business interests to convince President Hindenburg to sack Brüning.

May 1932: Von Schleicher selected von Papen, a wealthy politician, to head up the new government. Von Schleicher continued to influence events behind the scenes.

July 1932: In the elections, von Papen's coalition government lost seats. The Nazis increased their popular vote, winning 230 seats in the Reichstag. Hitler wanted Hindenburg to sack von Papen and make him the new chancellor. Hindenburg resisted as he thought Hitler was not suitable and from a low class of Germans.

November 1932: Von Papen called another election. The Nazi vote fell but they remained the largest party. The Nazis refused to give their support to von Papen. Powerful business leaders signed a letter to Hindenburg asking that Hitler be made chancellor, Hindenburg refused.

December 1932: Hindenburg appointed von Schleicher as chancellor. He asked Hindenburg to suspend the constitution and give him special powers as he believed von Papen and Hitler were trying to overthrow him. Hindenburg did not agree and news of von Schleicher's request meant he lost the support of the Reichstag.

January 1933: Hindenburg reluctantly appointed Hitler as chancellor.

EXAM-STYLE QUESTION

A01 **A02**

SKILLS PROBLEM SOLVING, REASONING, DECISION MAKING, ADAPTIVE LEARNING, INNOVATION

'The main reason that there was support for Hitler in the 1932 general election was because powerful interest groups in Germany underestimated Hitler's ambition.'

How far do you agree? Explain your answer.

You may use the following in your answer:
■ the November 1932 election result
■ the fears of industrialists.
You **must** also use information of your own. **(16 marks)**

HINT

Remember it is important to consider reasons for and against the statement. In this answer, you could also look at Hitler's popularity in the 1932 elections.

RECAP

RECALL QUIZ

1 Who founded the German Workers' Party in 1919?
2 What was Hitler's job at the end of the First World War?
3 What prison was Hitler sent to after the Munich Putsch?
4 What was the name of the book Hitler wrote while in prison?
5 What does the term *Lebensraum* mean?
6 Who was the leader of the SA?
7 When was Brüning chancellor?
8 What percentage of the vote did Hitler win in July 1932?
9 Why did Hindenburg dislike Hitler?
10 On what date did Hitler become chancellor?

CHECKPOINT

STRENGTHEN

S1 Explain three ways in which the Great Depression affected people in Germany.
S2 Explain three ways in which the Nazis used propaganda messages in their election campaigns.
S3 Explain how the role of the SA grew.

CHALLENGE

C1 Why did industrialists give their support to Hitler as chancellor?
C2 How far did the Nazis change their tactics to gain power after 1924?
C3 In what ways did the Weimar's weaknesses provide opportunities for Hitler?

SUMMARY

- The Nazi Party rose from being a minor political group in Munich to holding power in Germany.
- Under Hitler's leadership, the party was transformed. From 1924, the Nazis focused on using democratic means to get power.
- Until 1928, the Nazis remained a minor political party with very little influence.
- In the late 1920s, the economic situation in Germany changed dramatically due to the impact of the Wall Street Crash and the start of a worldwide economic depression. The Great Depression affected Germany particularly badly.
- The Nazis were in a position to take advantage of the economic crisis. They used extensive propaganda and intimidation to get more votes.
- The Weimar government was unable to find solutions to Germany's economic problems. Hitler benefited from the collapse of the Weimar democracy.
- Hitler was helped into power by powerful individuals in Germany who thought they could control him. He was also helped by business leaders, who preferred Hitler to the communist alternative.

EXAM GUIDANCE: PART (A) QUESTIONS

Study Extract A.

EXTRACT A

From a history of the modern world published in 2001.

Hitler used his trial to make long speeches and criticise the government. The publicity he received turned him into a national hero. Astonishingly, at the end of the trial Hitler was sentenced to just five years in prison and he was released after just nine months. Hitler now realised that power could best be achieved in Germany through the ballot box, rather than an armed uprising.

AO4

SKILLS ANALYSIS, INTERPRETATION, CEATIVITY

Question to be answered: What impression does the author give about attitudes in Germany at the time of Hitler's trial?

You **must** use Extract A to explain your answer.   (6 marks)

1 Analysis Question 1: What is the question type testing?
In this question, you have to analyse the extract and work out what impression the author set out to create. The key to answering this type of question is to understand that the author deliberately chooses how they write. They will make a choice about the language they use, the tone they adopt and the content they include to create a particular impression.

2 Analysis Question 2: What do I have to do to answer the question well?
You need to read the extract carefully and work out what the author is trying to make you think. Has the author set out to give a positive or negative impression? Are they trying to suggest that an event or policy was significant or insignificant, successful or unsuccessful, and so on?

3 Analysis Question 3: Are there any techniques I can use to make it very clear that I am doing what is needed to be successful?
This is a 6-mark question and you need to make sure you leave enough time to answer the other two questions fully (they are worth 24 marks in total). This is not an essay and you don't need to give a general introduction or conclusion. All you need to do is answer the question as quickly as you can.

A good way to do this is to state your answer straight away – for example: 'The impression the author is giving about Germany at this time is…'

Now you have to prove what you have said. You can do this by quoting from the answer, for example:
- 'I think this because of the language and tone…' Then quote from the extract to prove what you are saying about language and tone.
- 'I also think this because of the content the author has chosen…' Then quote from Extract A to prove what you are saying about content choice.

Answer A

The author of Extract A gives the impression that the publicity that Hitler received turned him into a national hero. He used his trial to make long speeches and criticise the government.

What are the strengths and weaknesses of Answer A?
Unfortunately, this is a very weak answer. The question asks about the impression given of Germany at the time, but the answer has simply copied parts of Extract A to say that Hitler became a national hero. This barely answers the question and would gain 1 or 2 marks at best.

Answer B

The author of Extract A gives the impression that at this time there was a great deal of sympathy for opponents of the Weimar Republic. We know this by what the author chooses to tell us about. We are told that Hitler made long speeches and was given only a short sentence (suggesting even the legal system was sympathetic to his views). Then we learn that Hitler now decided to use the ballot box to win power. So he must have thought Germans would support his anti-Weimar views. The language used shows that the author thinks that the sympathy shown towards Hitler at this time was surprising, because he says 'Astonishingly' Hitler got just a short sentence.

What are the strengths and weaknesses of Answer B?
This is a very good answer. It states the impression given and supports it with information from the extract. It also notes the use of language and it is concise and to the point.

Challenge a friend

Choose an extract from the Student Book and use it to set a part (a) question for a friend. Then look at the answer. Does it do the following things?

- ☐ State a valid impression from the extract
- ☐ Provide 3–4 lines explaining how language, tone and content choice prove this.

If it does, you can tell your friend that the answer is very good!

4. NAZI GERMANY 1933–39

LEARNING OBJECTIVES

- Understand the methods used by Hitler 1933–34 to create a dictatorship
- Understand the different methods of Nazi control and the extent to which they were successful
- Understand how Nazi policies affected life in Germany.

On 30 January 1933, Hitler was appointed chancellor of Germany. At this stage, Hitler was the leader of a democratic country. The government's powers were limited by the Weimar Constitution and there were regular elections, so the German electorate could remove politicians through peaceful means if they were dissatisfied with their leadership.

However, all this changed after 1933. Hitler destroyed democracy in Germany and replaced it with a dictatorship in which he was all-powerful. He used propaganda, censorship and police powers to influence and control the attitudes and behaviour of the German people. Nazi organisations – including the Gestapo, the SS and concentration camps – spread terror throughout Germany. Hitler also controlled all parts of Germany's culture, including religion, education, art and sport; this gave him even greater influence over people's attitudes and beliefs. Hitler and the Nazi Party brought about radical economic changes in Germany to address unemployment and prepare the country for war.

It was during this period that the Nazis began to oppress Jews in Germany and their lives became increasingly difficult in the years leading up to the Second World War.

4.1 SETTING UP THE NAZI DICTATORSHIP

LEARNING OBJECTIVES

- ☐ Understand the events and outcomes of the Reichstag fire and the Enabling Act
- ☐ Understand the causes of the Night of the Long Knives and the impact on Hitler's power
- ☐ Understand how Hitler became Führer.

27 February Reichstag fire

5 March Elections held; Nazis won 44% of the vote

14 July Law against forming new political parties

30 June Night of the Long Knives

30 January 1933 Hitler appointed chancellor

28 February Hindenburg used Article 48 to issue decrees

24 March Enabling Act passed

15 January 1934 State parliaments dissolved

2 August Hindenburg died and Hitler became head of state

By 30 January 1933, Hitler was the German chancellor. However, there were important limits to his powers.

- Under the Weimar Constitution, there were clear limits to the chancellor's powers to make laws.
- Hindenburg kept all the presidential powers.
- Hitler's cabinet of twelve included only two other Nazis.
- Only a third of the Reichstag members were Nazis.

Although Hitler was head of the government, his authority was dependent upon the support of other parties.

SOURCE A

A torchlight procession of Nazi Party supporters (including SA members) through the Brandenburg Gate. This procession took place on 30 January 1933 after Hitler was appointed Reich chancellor.

Some people in Germany were pleased that the Weimar Constitution limited the powers of extremist politicians such as Hitler. Many more Germans hated the Weimar Republic and blamed it for Germany's problems; they hoped Hitler would destroy it. Some politicians hoped that Hitler could be used to bring down the Weimar Republic. They then intended to replace him with a new leader of their choice. Most of these politicians underestimated Hitler, but some feared what Hitler might do. For example, Ludendorff (the First World War general who had helped Hitler to launch the Munich Putsch) clearly recognised the dangers, as shown in Source B. Ludendorff was right to be worried.

SOURCE B

Telegram from Ludendorff to President Hindenburg after Hitler's appointment as chancellor.

By appointing Hitler Chancellor of the Reich you have handed over our German Fatherland to one of the greatest troublemakers of all time. I predict this evil man will plunge our Reich into the abyss and will inflict immeasurable harm on our nation. Future generations will curse you in your grave for this action.

THE REICHSTAG FIRE

SOURCE C

From an account by a German general providing evidence about the Reichstag fire at the Nuremberg War Crimes Trial. This was the trial in which leading Nazis were prosecuted after the war.

At a luncheon on the birthday of Hitler in 1942 the conversation turned to the topic of the Reichstag building and its artistic value. I heard with my own ears when Goering interrupted the conversation and shouted: 'The only one who really knows about the Reichstag is I, because I set it on fire!' With that he slapped his thigh with the flat of his hand.

On the evening of 27 February 1933, the Reichstag building was destroyed by fire. A Dutch communist, Marinus van der Lubbe, was found on the site with matches and firelighters. He confessed to starting the fire and was put on trial alongside four other men. Van der Lubbe insisted that he had acted alone; he was found guilty and executed by **guillotine** on 9 January 1934. The other three men were acquitted.

There is considerable doubt about whether van der Lubbe really was responsible for the fire. Some historians believe he was set up by the Nazis to start the fire; others believe the Nazis started the fire themselves and blamed it on van der Lubbe. The only clear fact is that van der Lubbe was a communist. The Nazis used this to their advantage.

ACTIVITY

1 Study Source B.
   a What was Ludendorff saying about Hitler?
   b Why do you think Hindenburg didn't dismiss Hitler at this point?
2 Study Source C. Are you surprised by what this source says? Explain your answer.

CONSEQUENCES OF THE FIRE

The new Nazi chief of police was a man called Hermann Goering. He said that van der Lubbe had been part of a communist anti-government plot and the Nazis should seize this opportunity to destroy communist opposition. Hitler used the fire to attack the Communists and increase his own personal power. On the night of the fire, 4,000 communist leaders were arrested. On 28 February, Hitler persuaded Hindenburg to pass a new emergency decree – the 'Decree for the Protection of the People and State'. This gave police the power to search homes and imprison anyone they arrested without trial. The police were also able to ban meetings and close newspapers and Goering used the decree to take over the state radio station.

THE MARCH 1933 ELECTION

EXTEND YOUR KNOWLEDGE

VAN DER LUBBE'S PARDON

Van der Lubbe was beheaded by guillotine in 1934. However, a law passed in 1998 set out new rules for people who had committed crimes while the Nazis were in power. This law argued that Nazi law itself went against the true principles of justice. In 2008, van der Lubbe was pardoned by the German government.

Shortly after becoming chancellor, Hitler called an election for a new Reichstag. The elections were on 5 March 1933, just 6 days after the Reichstag fire. Hitler was determined to secure more seats in the Reichstag for the Nazis. He claimed that the Reichstag fire was proof of a serious communist threat, and that people should vote for the Nazis to stop this threat. He also took various other steps before the elections, to try to ensure the Nazis would do well.

- Goering began to replace police officers with Nazi supporters. He also recruited 50,000 SA members to be 'police auxiliaries'. Hitler was effectively in control of the police force, so SA violence – for example, to intimidate opponents – was not stopped. During the election campaign, political violence led to around 70 deaths.
- Thousands of members of the Communist Party and the Social Democratic Party were arrested and sent to concentration camps.
- The SA broke up election meetings by opposition parties.
- Newspapers which did not support the Nazis were closed.
- Hitler secured funds from industrialists to help the Nazi election campaign. They gave generously because the Nazis promised to destroy communism and ensure stability in Germany.
- The Nazis issued huge quantities of propaganda.
- Threatening supporters were posted at polling stations to encourage 'correct' voting.

These measures enabled the Nazis to win many new seats in the Reichstag. However, Hitler was disappointed by the result. Although the Nazis were now the largest party in the Reichstag, they did not have a majority. This meant their measures could be voted down by other parties.

▶ **Figure 4.1** Election results, 5 March 1933

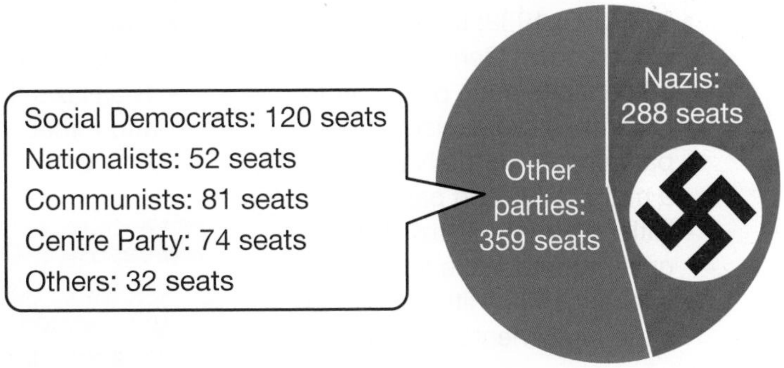

Social Democrats: 120 seats
Nationalists: 52 seats
Communists: 81 seats
Centre Party: 74 seats
Others: 32 seats

Other parties: 359 seats

Nazis: 288 seats

Hitler had hoped to gain two-thirds of the seats in the Reichstag. This would allow him to make changes to the German constitution. Hitler wanted to bring in a new law which would give him unlimited powers and allow him to pass laws without asking the Reichstag. If he did not have a two-thirds majority yet, he would have to find a way to get one.

THE ENABLING ACT

In the weeks following the election, Hitler worked hard to persuade the other parties to support his new law.
- He used the emergency powers to ban the Communist Party members (81 seats) from the Reichstag.
- The Nationalist Party (52 seats) agreed to support him, because many of their beliefs were similar to those of the Nazis.
- He won support from the Centre Party (74 seats) by promising to protect the **Catholic** Church.

SOURCE D

A member of the Social Democratic Party describes the scene just before the vote on the Enabling Act.

The place was crawling with armed SA and SS men. The assembly hall was decorated with swastikas. When we Social Democrats had taken our seats SA and SS men lined up at the exits and along the walls behind us in a semi-circle. Their expressions did not bode well… Later when we tried to interrupt Hitler the SA and SS people hissed loudly and murmured 'Shut up', 'Traitors', 'You'll be hung today'.

With this support, Hitler had the majority he needed – as long as the other parties kept their promises. To ensure this happened, Hitler placed the SA and SS around the Reichstag to intimidate members; the presence of these soldiers would also persuade the Social Democratic Party to vote for the new law. After a short debate, the vote was taken. The 'Enabling Act' was passed by 444 votes to 94.

CONSEQUENCES OF THE ENABLING ACT

The Enabling Act marked an end to the Weimar Constitution and the end of democracy itself in Germany. This act allowed Hitler to make laws and to sign treaties with foreign powers without the approval of the Reichstag. The original act applied for 4 years, but it was renewed in 1937. For the rest of Hitler's time in power, the Reichstag met only 12 times. When the Reichstag did meet, its role was no longer to debate or make decisions. Instead, it was there to listen to Hitler making speeches.

Hitler no longer needed Reichstag approval to make decisions. He used his new powers to remove any remaining opposition to his government; this became known as 'the Nazi Revolution'. The main targets of this revolution were local government, the trade unions and other political parties. Hitler wanted to weaken the trade unions because they had communist sympathies and many workers were loyal to their union rather than to Nazism. The Nazis also wanted to win the favour of big businesses, which were keen to see the power of the trade unions reduced. The key measures by which Hitler removed opposition are outlined in Figure 4.2.

Measure 1: Local government
- 31 March 1933: the Nazis closed down Germany's 18 separate state parliaments.
- Hitler then reorganised these parliaments so the Nazis held a majority in each parliament.
- Hitler appointed Nazi state governors to make laws.
- January 1934: Hitler abolished state parliaments altogether.

Measure 2: Trade unions
- 2 May 1933: the Nazis broke into the trade union offices and arrested their leaders.
- The Nazis then created the German Workers' Front, and forced workers to join this new organisation.

Measure 3: Other political parties
- 10 May 1933: the Social Democrats were suspended. The Nazis occupied their party offices and took their funds.
- End of May 1933: the Nazis suspended the Communist Party in the same way.
- July 1933: Hitler created a new law which banned all political parties except the Nazi Party.

▶ **Figure 4.2** Measures to remove opposition after the Enabling Act was passed in March 1933

EXAM-STYLE QUESTION

A01 **A02**

Explain **two** effects on Germany of Hitler's Enabling Act.   **(8 marks)**

HINT

You will want to look at Figure 4.2 before answering this question. Remember to explain the effects by concentrating on how things were now different.

NIGHT OF THE LONG KNIVES: 30 JUNE 1934

The SA had played a major part in helping the Nazis rise to power. By 1934, however, Hitler felt it was time to reduce the power of the SA. There were many reasons for this.

■ The SA was becoming very powerful; in 1934, it had over 2 million members. Its leader, Ernst Röhm, was a possible rival to Hitler as leader of the Nazi Party.

■ The head of the SS, Heinrich Himmler, resented the SA's influence and was keen to reduce its importance.

■ Some SA members continued to use violence and intimidation and their behaviour was an embarrassment to Hitler. In addition, there were frequent drunken fights between SA members. As a result, the Nazis lost the support of many conservative Germans.

■ Röhm had very different views to Hitler. Röhm wanted to take measures against big businesses and adopt socialist policies. Hitler wanted the support of the business leaders in Germany – and the funding that would come with it.

■ Some people in the Nazi Party were offended by Röhm's homosexuality and believed he was 'corrupting' the Hitler Youth.

■ Perhaps most importantly, the influence of the SA affected the Nazis' relations with the regular army. As a result of the Treaty of Versailles, the army had only 100,000 men. Despite this, the army leaders were influential men. Hitler had plans to rearm Germany and increase the size of its army, but the SA wanted to take the place of the army. In 1934, SA units began stopping army convoys and confiscating their weapons. Hitler felt he had to take action.

On 30 June 1934, Hitler launched what became known as the Night of the Long Knives. Members of the SS arrested around 200 SA officers. These officers were taken to Munich, where many of them – including Röhm – were executed. We do not know for certain how many died, but it is believed to be around 90. The SA leaders were not the only targets. Hitler also took revenge on old enemies like von Kahr and Schleicher, and removed a possible rival for Nazi leadership, Gregor Strasser. Hitler was more than happy to take responsibility for the events of that night. He claimed he was defending Germany against a plot that was going to be led by Röhm.

The German people reacted in various ways to the Night of the Long Knives, as shown in Figure 4.3 and in Sources E, F and Extract A.

EXTEND YOUR KNOWLEDGE

ERNST RÖHM

Hitler and Röhm had a long-standing friendship until Hitler ordered his execution in 1934. Röhm's private life was not in the Nazi tradition. He was a heavy drinker of alcohol and was openly homosexual. After the Night of the Long Knives he refused to commit suicide, saying, 'Hitler can kill me himself'. He was shot in prison. Röhm had featured in a 1933 propaganda film, *The Victory of Faith*. In an attempt to write Röhm out of German history, Hitler ordered the destruction of all copies of this film.

SA

We have been weakened by these events. Our leader has been murdered and our power has been reduced.

SS

We have shown Hitler our loyalty by helping him to carry out these murders. We are now independent of the SA and under Hitler's personal command.

Hitler

I now have total loyalty from the army as they have to swear a personal oath to me. All my opponents fear me now.

Opponent

I was right. Hitler is a murderer and we now live in terror.

Supporter

Hitler only did this to protect us from Germany's enemies. It shows he has the courage to protect us, even from people who were his friends in the past.

▲ **Figure 4.3** Reactions to the Night of the Long Knives

SOURCE E

A cartoon from a British newspaper, 3 July 1934. The caption was 'They salute with both hands now' and Hitler's armband says 'The Double Cross'.

THEY SALUTE WITH BOTH HANDS NOW.

SOURCE F

Hitler's address to the Reichstag, broadcast on the radio on 13 July 1934.

If anyone asks me why I did not use the regular courts of justice for conviction of the offenders, then all I can say to him is this: in this hour I was responsible for the fate of the German people and became the supreme judge of the German people.

ACTIVITY

1 Study Source E.
   a What is the cartoonist's view of Hitler's actions?
   b What techniques does the cartoonist use to put his message across?
2 Read Source F. Do you think the German people would have been reassured or worried by what Hitler said? Explain your answer.

EXTRACT A

An extract from a modern history book about the Night of the Long Knives.

The greatest winner of all was Hitler. He had gained the acceptance of the legalised murder of opponents. Most Germans accepted the view that, as their Führer, he would only act for the good of the nation. The Night of the Long Knives showed that the rule of law was to be replaced by the decisions of one man… [who] had a horrific vision of the future.

EXAM-STYLE QUESTION

AO4

SKILLS ANALYSIS, INTERPRETATION, CREATIVITY

Study Extract A.
What impression does the author give about the importance of the Night of the Long Knives in Germany?

You **must** use Extract A to explain your answer.   **(6 marks)**

HINT

Remember to back up your points by using short direct quotes from the extract in your answer.

HITLER BECOMES FÜHRER

KEY TERMS

Third Reich Germany's third **empire**. The first two had been the Holy Roman Empire (800 to 1806) and the German Empire of 1871 to 1918 (the Second Reich)

plebiscite a public vote on a single issue, rather than an election for a leader

On 2 August 1934, President Hindenburg died aged 84. Hitler took the opportunity to increase his power. He combined the offices of chancellor and president and declared himself 'Führer' (leader) of Germany. Hitler was now firmly in control of what became known as the **Third Reich**.

From now on, the army loyalty **oath** was made to him directly, rather than to Germany. This meant that the army swore to obey him personally if there was a struggle for power, rather than accepting the orders of their military commanders. Hitler held a **plebiscite** to get the public to agree to all these changes. Following a huge Nazi propaganda campaign, Hitler gained 90 per cent of the public vote.

SOURCE G

Swearing-in of new army recruits, 1935.

4.2 NAZI METHODS OF CONTROL

LEARNING OBJECTIVES

- Understand how the Nazis set up a police state in Germany
- Understand the use of censorship and propaganda for controlling opposition
- Understand Nazi policies towards education, women and the young.

KEY TERMS

the Church meaning the organisation, not the building; in Germany, there was the Catholic Church and the Protestant Church (each with several different Churches)

indoctrination forcing people to accept certain ideas by offering no alternatives

censorship official suppression of certain information, such as books, art or newspapers

police state a totalitarian state controlled by a police force which watches people to make sure they do not oppose the government

Gestapo *Geheime Staatspolizei*: secret police whose role was to find enemies of the Nazi state

Hitler had established himself as the unchallenged leader of Germany. Now, he set about ensuring the Nazis would remain in power, using a variety of methods. Many people in Germany shared Hitler's ideas, so he would have their support. But how would he deal with those who did not support him? The answer was simple.

Hitler's rule would be **totalitarian**: he would have control over all aspects of peoples' lives. This meant there would be very little opportunity for opposition. Germany would be a one-party state, with all political institutions run by members of the Nazi Party. The Nazis also controlled the police, the courts, radio and newspapers, education, films, the Arts, trade unions, the **Churches** and working conditions. They even told German women that it was 'un-German' to use products to change hair colour or to wear make-up.

Nazi rule would also involve **indoctrination**, **censorship** and propaganda to win people over to Nazi beliefs. There were rewards for 'good Nazis'. For example, women who had a large number of babies were given medals, while good workers might be rewarded with cheap tickets to the theatre.

Beneath the control and the propaganda, however, there was a policy of terror. Germany was a **police state**: the SS and **Gestapo** clamped down on any opposition and the courts usually found defendants guilty. The first concentration camp opened in 1933 and soon there was a network of camps across Germany. People suspected of opposing Nazi rule were often imprisoned in these camps.

TERROR AND THE POLICE STATE

A police state is a totalitarian state in which the government uses the police to control the population. Hitler was determined to remove any opposition to his rule. He introduced a series of measures to ensure that most Germans were too frightened even to criticise the Nazis.

- Under Hitler, German law became whatever the Nazi Party believed was right. Germans could be arrested and imprisoned without trial. The Nazis created a new central court, called the People's Court; they also established new 'Special Courts' across Germany. These courts had no juries and the judges were expected to support Nazi policies. There was no right of appeal against a sentence. Many political opponents were sentenced to death by these courts and executed.

- There were a number of different police forces in Germany but, in 1936, the SS and Gestapo were brought together under Himmler's command. Himmler was a strong believer in 'racial and moral purity': between 1933 and 1935, he had dismissed 60,000 SS members for being homosexuals, **alcoholics** or 'morally corrupt', showing the power of the Nazi police state.

- The SS was responsible for identifying and arresting political prisoners and for running the concentration camps in Germany.
- The Gestapo was responsible for state security. A huge number of informers reported to the Gestapo; for example, every block of flats had a block leader who would report any suspicious behaviour or criticism of the government. The Gestapo often handed suspects over to the SS to be **tortured**. However, not all Germans believed they were being oppressed or, if they did, they felt the benefits were more important than the loss of personal freedom. This helps to explain why thousands of Germans were willing to help the Gestapo by informing on people they knew.
- Most people suspected of opposition to the Nazis were sent to prison or to the concentration camps. In these camps, inmates were forced to work, and torture and brutality were common. It has been estimated that over 200,000 Germans were imprisoned for showing supposed opposition to Nazi rule. Some of these people were arrested after a new law was passed – the Law on Malicious Gossip. This made it illegal even to tell jokes about Hitler.

The key forms of Nazi terror and control are outlined in Figure 4.4.

The SS

This organisation started out as Hitler's personal bodyguard.

In 1932, they introduced a new black uniform with a silver badge; this made them stand out from other uniformed Nazis.

Under Himmler's leadership, the SS grew to hundreds of thousands, with local branches across Germany. The SS could arrest anyone they wanted, and execute or detain them without trial.

Concentration camps

These were originally used to hold political prisoners. Early camps were based in disused factories or warehouses. Over time, a network of camps was put in place.

Prisoners were treated harshly; they were often worked to death or died of disease. The camp system was run by the SS, who were responsible for protecting the Reich and carrying out Hitler's racial policies.

The Gestapo

The Gestapo had the power to search anyone's home. They appointed local block wardens to watch their neighbours and report any suspicious activity. By 1942, the Gestapo had around 30,000 officers.

Informers

The Gestapo relied heavily on ordinary Germans who voluntarily informed on other people in their area. Most historians agree that at least half of all Gestapo investigations came about because of information provided by neighbours, colleagues, friends or even family members.

▶ **Figure 4.4** Nazi terror and control

ACTIVITY

1 List three ways in which the Nazis used terror to control people in Germany.
2 How did the Nazis create a police state?

EXTEND YOUR KNOWLEDGE

CARL VON OSSIETZKY

Carl von Ossietzky was a German pacifist who was an opponent of the Nazi regime. He was arrested in 1933 and spent the next 5 years in Gestapo custody. In 1935, he was awarded the Nobel Peace Prize and his supporters said the awarding committee should 'send the Peace Prize into the concentration camp'. Hitler was angered by the award, calling it an insult to Germany. He said that no German would ever be allowed to accept a Nobel Prize. Von Ossietzky's health was weakened by the poor treatment he received in concentration camps and he died in 1938.

CENSORSHIP AND PROPAGANDA

The Nazis knew that their terror **tactics** would prevent opposition to their rule. However, it would be better for them if they could create a society where people supported the Nazis because they believed in their policies and wanted to see them implemented. Joseph Goebbels had been made Minister of Propaganda and National Enlightenment in 1933. He was given the task of winning over the hearts and minds of the German people (see Figure 4.5). He used censorship and propaganda to do this.

- Hitler made him Minister of Enlightenment and Propaganda in 1933.
- He co-ordinated Nazi policy towards the media, sport, culture and the arts.
- He promoted Nazi beliefs and attitudes through propaganda.
- He believed propaganda should be subtle: people should come to believe Nazi ideas without realising they were being targeted by propaganda messages.

▶ **Figure 4.5** Joseph Goebbels

CENSORSHIP

If the German people were to live their lives according to Nazi beliefs, it was important that they read or heard only the 'correct message'. The Nazis used censorship to ensure this happened.

- Newspapers were strictly controlled and any paper that opposed the Nazis was shut down. Editors were made responsible for ensuring there were no critical articles in their publications. All owners, editors and journalists had to be members of the Reich Press Chamber, and no one with unacceptable views could become a member of this chamber.
- Programmes on the radio were strictly controlled. In 1934, all radio stations in Germany were brought together under the Reich Radio Company. Radios made in Germany could not pick up foreign broadcasts.
- The Ministry of Propaganda made a list of unacceptable literature and the Gestapo had the power to search bookshops and libraries and seize such publications. Students were encouraged to burn books that portrayed 'un-German' views (see Source H). Millions of books from universities and libraries were burned in Nazi-organised rallies. Any authors who were anti-Nazi, communist or Jewish were banned.
- Censorship also extended to the arts. All writers, actors and musicians had to join the Reich Chamber of Commerce (established by Goebbels). If their work was considered unsuitable, they were left out and could not work. Some types of music were banned, including anything that was influenced by American culture. Jazz was banned because it was seen as black music, and therefore inferior and unsuitable for Aryans. Art that showed Nazi values, including Aryan Germans, was encouraged, while other forms of art were banned. Hitler had a particular hatred for modern art, saying it damaged Germany and weakened Nazism.

EXTEND YOUR KNOWLEDGE

EXHIBITION OF DEGENERATE ART 1937

The Exhibition of Degenerate Art was organised by the Nazis. It included pieces by international artists whose work the Nazis disapproved of. The exhibition handbook showed how the pictures represented views that were damaging to Germany. The exhibition was intended to encourage negative feeling towards the art. Pictures were hung badly, with graffiti on the walls, insulting the artists. Despite this, the exhibition attracted five times as many visitors as an exhibition of 'approved' art that took place at the same time.

SOURCE H

Book burning in Berlin in May 1933. 'Un-German' literature was burned in many German university towns. These events were arranged by the German Student Association's Office for Press and Propaganda.

SOURCE I

Orange by Wasily Kandinsky, 1923.

SOURCE J

Venus and Adonis by Arthur Kampf, 1939.

ACTIVITY

1 The Nazis banned the art in Source I but approved of the art in Source J. Match the statements to the paintings in Source I and Source J.
 - Shows Aryan strength and beauty
 - Concept art that challenges tradition
 - German warrior and protector
 - Disrupts common ideas about ordinary things

Now think of two more statements of your own.

2 Write a paragraph to explain the type of art Hitler liked.

EXAM-STYLE QUESTION

A01   **A02**

Explain **two** effects on Germany of Nazi censorship.   **(8 marks)**

HINT

Make sure you remember to explain the impact of censorship. Don't just describe types of censorship in Germany.

PROPAGANDA

The Nazis used censorship to make sure people in Germany received no 'un-German' messages. At the same time, they used propaganda to spread positive messages about the Nazi Party and to encourage people to share the Nazi view of what it meant to be German. The key messages of Nazi propaganda were:

 - the supremacy of the Aryan race and the inferiority of the Jews and other races
 - the tremendous work being done by the Nazis to deal with the evils of communism

- the different roles of men and women in society and the importance of family
- the fact that all citizens had a duty to suffer for the good of the nation.

Hitler believed propaganda should repeat Nazi messages in simple terms, using power and emotion. Goebbels believed that propaganda would be more effective if people did not realise they were being manipulated. He felt propaganda messages should be more subtle.

- Newspapers were used to 'plant' stories and present positive Nazi messages (Source K). The Ministry of Propaganda gave daily orders to newspaper editors, telling them what stories to publish. The state-controlled news agency often produced the articles and newspapers simply had to print them, without any changes.
- Hitler saw the radio as his most important propaganda aid. Factories were encouraged to produce cheap radio sets and, by 1939, 70 per cent of German households had a radio. Goebbels believed propaganda was most effective if people did not realise it was propaganda. He issued plays and light entertainment that subtly included Nazi messages.
- Owners of factories, bars and restaurants were ordered to install loudspeaker systems so they could broadcast Hitler's speeches.
- The Nazis used public parades and rallies as a form of propaganda. On national holidays, parades were held in most German towns and citizens were expected to hang out swastika flags. The huge Nuremberg rallies, often lit by torches, showed the power and glory of Germany under the Nazis.
- In the years after the Wall Street Crash, posters had played a key role in advertising Nazi views. The Nazis continued to use them after they took power. Posters were particularly useful in portraying Hitler as a great leader who could do no wrong (Source L).
- The arts were used to promote Nazi values. Films reflected the Nazi view on society and a visit to the cinema usually included pro-Nazi newsreels. The music of Bach, Beethoven and Mozart was played regularly, as were marching songs and German folk songs. Art was expected to show heroic German figures and promote the Aryan race and family values. Art had flourished during the Weimar period, but Hitler dismissed much of this as 'degenerate'.
- In 1936, the Olympic Games were held in Berlin. The Nazis used this as an opportunity to show the world the supremacy of the Aryan race. At this time, German schools emphasised the importance of sport and this was reflected in the fact that Germany won more medals than any other country. The major disappointment for Hitler was that the star athlete of the games was not an Aryan: Jesse Owens – a black American – won four gold medals.

SOURCE K

Instructions given to the press by the Ministry of Propaganda and National Enlightenment in 1939, 2 days before war began.

In the next edition there must be a lead article, featured as prominently as possible, in which the decision of the Führer, no matter what it will be, will be discussed as the only correct one for Germany.

SOURCE L

SOURCE L

A Nazi poster from the 1930s entitled 'Long Live Germany'.

ACTIVITY

1 What is the difference between censorship and propaganda? Give three examples of each.
2 What was the purpose of the poster in Source L? How does it try to achieve this?

NAZI POLICIES TOWARDS EDUCATION, WOMEN AND YOUNG PEOPLE

YOUNG PEOPLE AND EDUCATION

The Nazis saw education as an opportunity to indoctrinate young people, to ensure they grew up to be loyal Nazis. Hitler believed that young peoples' minds were open to influence and control and he took advantage of this. School curricula were changed to emphasise Nazi ideas. Outside school hours, young people were expected to attend Nazi youth groups – the Nazis wanted to reduce the amount of time children spent with their families, to limit other influences on their beliefs and attitudes. Hitler wanted to ensure the next generation met Nazi ideals.

Teachers were forced to join the Nazi teachers' association or lose their jobs. Many teachers attended Nazi training camps, where they learned how to pass on Nazi values to the children in their care. The curriculum was changed and textbooks were rewritten to reflect Nazi beliefs. All new books had to be checked and approved by Nazi officials.

The school curriculum

New subjects were created and the focus of other subjects was changed. For example:

■ 'Race Studies' (a new subject) taught young people that Aryans were superior and that Jews were the lowest racial type.

■ More time was given to PE (physical education), so children would remain fit and healthy. This would prepare the boys to become soldiers and the girls to become mothers.

■ Examples in mathematics often used military problems, such as the distance of targets for bombing attacks.

■ In history, children learned about the rise of the Nazi Party.

■ The biology curriculum emphasised the supremacy of the Aryans.

■ In geography, children were taught about the German need for *Lebensraum*, or living space.

■ Domestic science was taught to female students only, to prepare them for their futures as wives and mothers.

SOURCE M

An illustration titled 'Trust No Fox on the Heath and No Jew on his Word'. From a book used to teach young children about Jews in Germany, 1935.

ACTIVITY

Study Source M.

1 How are Aryans shown in the children's book?

2 How are Jews shown?

3 What is the message to young children about different racial groups?

Hitler Leadership schools

The Nazis set up some extra schools, to educate boys for future leadership in the Reich. Some Nazi organisations, including the SS, ran schools that were designed to train boys to become military leaders, so they could help to run the Nazi state administration when they grew up. The boys were given physical and political training to prepare them for their future roles.

NAZI YOUTH MOVEMENTS

Before 1933, there were many youth groups in Germany; these were often run by churches or by other political parties. In 1926, the Nazis had founded the Hitler Youth but its membership was small. In 1933, the Nazis banned all other youth groups (except, at first, those in the Catholic Church). In 1936, the Hitler Youth Law was passed. Under this law, all eligible young people had to belong to a Nazi youth organisation, although there were no penalties for non-membership. In 1939, this law became stricter and membership became compulsory. Figure 4.6 shows the different groups for boys and girls.

Children spent evenings and weekends at Hitler Youth meetings. This time was spent learning about Hitler and how he had saved Germany from the communist traitors. Hitler Youth members discussed political pamphlets and ideas and performed military drills. They were also taught about the importance of competition and racial **purity**. Groups for girls emphasised crafts and childcare, to prepare the girls for motherhood. Activities were made fun – for example, summer camps and physical activities – so that young people would enjoy being part of the Nazi movement. Hitler Youth members were encouraged to report anyone who they believed was not loyal to the Nazi state, even their own parents. By 1939, 8 million young people were members.

Young German Folk
Boys aged 10–14

German Young Girls
Girls aged 10–14

Hitler Youth
Boys aged 14–18

League of German Maidens
Girls aged 14–18

▲ **Figure 4.6** Nazi Youth organisations that recruited girls and boys aged 10–18 years

EXTRACT B

From a modern history book on Nazi Germany.

Through the training of young men and women, the Nazis hoped to create the new men and women of the People's Germany. What National Socialist training produced, however, were duller and stupider, though healthier individuals.

EXAM-STYLE QUESTION

AO4

SKILLS ANALYSIS, INTERPRETATION, CREATIVITY

Study Extract B.

What impression does the author give about the impact of Nazi youth policies on Germany?

You **must** use Extract B to explain your answer.

(6 marks)

> **HINT**
>
> Remember to focus on the impact of the youth policies. Don't just describe the changes the Nazis made to education.

WOMEN

During the 1920s, women had played an increasingly important role in German society. Many women were employed in jobs such as teachers, doctors and civil servants, and 10 per cent of the members of the Reichstag were women. When the Nazis came to power, they wanted to stop this. The birth rate in Germany was falling, so the government wanted to encourage women to stay at home and have babies.

- The Nazis launched a huge propaganda campaign to encourage women to have more children. Contraception and abortion were banned and the joys of having a large family were emphasised (Source O).
- In 1933, the Law for Encouragement of Marriage provided loans to help young couples marry – but only if the woman gave up work.
- Medals were awarded to women with large families (gold for eight children, silver for six and bronze for five).
- The German Women's Enterprise Organisation trained women in household skills.

The Nazi message was not entirely focused on babies. It also reflected a belief in older 'traditional' attitudes to women. For example, women were encouraged not to use make-up and to wear home-produced clothes and flat heels. Smoking and drinking were discouraged as they were 'unladylike' (not feminine); in addition, they might harm women's health and make it harder for them to have children. Slimming was also discouraged because it was believed that larger women found it easier to give birth.

However, Nazi policies towards women created economic problems. As the rearmament policy grew, there was a need for more workers – especially as more men joined the army. The Nazis had to relax the limits on women working (such as the marriage loans scheme) and encourage women back into work. By 1939, the number of women working was 50 per cent higher than it had been in 1933.

The table opposite shows how women's roles changed under the Nazis.

	WOMEN IN WEIMAR GERMANY	WOMEN IN NAZI GERMANY
Politics	All women over 20 years old had the right to vote in elections. By 1933, 10% of Reichstag members were women – this was advanced compared to other European nations and was a sign of increasing equality for women.	Hitler wanted women to focus on the home and family; he believed they should not have a role in politics. The Nazis wanted women to increase the population by having lots of babies.
Appearance	Female fashions included shorter skirts, trousers and make-up.	Women were expected to wear traditional dress and promote 'racial purity'. Make-up was discouraged.
Work	Many German women had professional careers and some earned as much as men.	Women were removed from paid employment; this helped to reduce unemployment figures and pushed women back into domestic roles. Later, however, women were encouraged to return to work.
Freedom	Young women could go out without an escort and it was socially acceptable for women to drink and smoke in public places.	Women were expected to keep themselves healthy so they could produce lots of children. Smoking and drinking were seen as unladylike.
Family and children	Women had access to contraception and many chose to have smaller families.	Women were expected to have large families and women who had lots of children were rewarded with medals called the Honour Cross. The Nazis made contraception and abortions illegal.

SOURCE N

A speech by Hitler to the Nazi Women's Organisation.

The woman's is a smaller world. For her world is her husband, her family, her children, and her home... the greater world is built on this smaller one... These worlds belong together just as a man and a woman belong together... To the one belongs the strength of feeling. To the other belongs the strength of vision, of making tough decisions.

SOURCE O

A stamp from Nazi Germany showing the ideal Aryan family.

ACTIVITY

Study Sources N and O. What do the sources tell you about Nazi attitudes towards women?

4.3 THE IMPACT OF NAZI DOMESTIC POLICIES

LEARNING OBJECTIVES

- Understand how Nazi policies affected the Churches
- Understand how German racial policies led to persecution of the Jews
- Understand persecution of the Jews up to 1939.

THE CHURCHES

The Nazis were determined to control what Germans heard at school or on the radio; they also wanted to ensure everyone was aware of the benefits of a state run according to Nazi principles. They knew that the Churches in Germany could have a major impact on people's attitudes, so they made sure they were 'brought into line' with Nazi ideas.

In Germany, the majority of the population was **Christian**; two-thirds were **Protestant** and about a third were **Roman Catholic**. Hitler wanted to replace religion in Germany with Nazism, but he knew that some of the principles of Nazism went against Christian beliefs. The Churches in Germany fully supported his views on the family, but some of his views (such as his racial beliefs) brought him into conflict with the Churches. Hitler knew he had to take care not to offend people's religious beliefs. He therefore took control of the Churches in a gradual and careful way.

THE CATHOLIC CHURCH

Catholics were loyal to the **Pope** as the head of the Catholic Church. Hitler wanted all Germans to see him as the supreme head of state, so he was keen to weaken the power and authority of the Catholic Church in Germany. Some Catholics preferred Catholic Youth groups and Catholic schools to those run by the German state. This reduced the Nazis' influence. Hitler was determined to increase his influence over the Catholics.

At first, Hitler and the Catholic Church tried to co-operate with each other. Hitler wanted the support of the Catholics and, in turn, the Catholic Church wanted to show its support for the country. In 1933, the concordat was signed. This was an agreement that stated that the Church would not get involved in political affairs and the Nazis would allow the Catholic Church to have freedom of worship and to run its own youth groups and schools.

Hitler soon broke this agreement. In schools, Christian symbols were taken down. Hitler wanted his own image to appear in classrooms, rather than the crucifix (the Christian cross symbol). Catholic newspapers were censored and propaganda began to hint at financial **corruption** in the Church. In 1937, Pope Pius XI tried to make a stand. He made a statement which attacked the Nazi criticism of the Catholic Church. This statement was read out by priests in all German Catholic churches. The Nazi reaction was severe.

- Membership of the Catholic League (the youth group for Catholic young people) was made illegal. Hitler wanted all young people to attend Hitler Youth groups instead.

- State funding for the Church was cut and the property of some monasteries was seized.
- Gestapo and SS agents began to spy on Church organisations.
- Catholic Church schools were closed and turned into community schools.
- Catholic priests who spoke out against the Nazis were arrested. Some priests were held in concentration camps.

Hitler had asserted his authority over the Catholic Church, but it continued to function. The number of people going to church remained high, despite Nazi attempts to weaken its influence.

THE PROTESTANT CHURCH

Many Protestants in Germany were nationalists and some agreed strongly with Nazi beliefs. One group, the 'German Christians', actually referred to itself as the 'SA of the Church'. They combined Nazi symbols and customs with Christian practices, wore Nazi uniforms and gave the Nazi salute at church services.

In 1933, Hitler organised all the different parts of the Protestant Church into one organisation, called the Reich Church. Ludwig Müller, a supporter of the Nazis, was made Bishop of the Reich Church. Under pressure from the German Christians, 18 pastors lost their jobs because they would not declare their support for Nazi views.

SOURCE P

Newly-appointed Reich Bishop Ludwig Müller, surrounded by supporting members of the SS and SA in September 1933.

SOURCE Q

Hitler in a private conversation in 1933.

I will make peace with the church. Why not! It won't stop me ridding Christianity from Germany completely. You are either Christian or German. You can't be both.

ACTIVITY

Write a discussion between a Catholic priest and a Protestant pastor to show their concerns about the actions of the Nazis towards the Churches in 1933.

However, there was some resistance to the Nazis' attempts to take control of the Protestant Church in Germany. A group of pastors, led by Martin Niemoller and Dietrich Bonhoeffer, set up the Confessional Church in 1934. This Church grew until it had 5,000 members and became a rival to the official Reich Church. The Confessional Church objected to the Nazis trying to interfere in matters of its religious faith; it said the Church should remain independent from Nazi political powers. As a result, Niemoller and hundreds of other Protestant clergy were sent to concentration camps. Bonhoeffer was hanged in 1945.

By the end of the 1930s, neither the Catholic Church nor the Protestant Church had a significant role in society. This was a result of Nazi measures, such as the introduction of the Hitler Youth, the banning of church schools and the use of propaganda against the Churches. In 1939, only 5 per cent of the German population described themselves as 'God-believers'.

NAZI RACIAL POLICIES AND JEWISH PERSECUTION

KEY TERMS

Untermenschen the German word for sub-humans or inferior humans

intermarriage marriage between different racial groups

Nazism was based on a world view in which different racial or **ethnic** groups were seen as either superior or inferior. Hitler said that the Aryan race was the ideal – blond hair, blue eyes, tall and athletic. He said that other groups, particularly Jews and **Gypsies**, were sub-human and did not deserve to be alive. He called them *Untermenschen*. Hitler wanted Germans to help build an Aryan master race. People who could not contribute were seen as a problem that needed to be dealt with.

The Nazis made the following changes to remove those who were considered a burden on society.

- In 1933, a Sterilisation Law was passed. This allowed the Nazis to **sterilise** people with illnesses such as 'simple-mindedness' (mental disability). From September 1933, tramps and beggars were also sterilised. It is believed that up to 700,000 people were sterilised by the Nazis.
- From 1936, **juvenile delinquents**, tramps, homosexuals and Jews were sent to concentration camps. From 1938, gypsies were also sent to these camps. Although there were only 30,000 gypsies in Germany, the Nazis did not want them mixing with Aryans. In 1935, **intermarriage** between gypsies and Germans was banned. In 1938, a decree for the 'Struggle against the Gypsy Plague' forced gypsies to register with the state.
- The Nazis believed that mental illness was **hereditary**. At first, people with mental illnesses were sterilised but, from 1939, the Nazis began to put them to death instead – first by starvation or **lethal injection** and later using **gas chambers**. This policy was abandoned in 1941, following public protests but, by this time, over 70,000 people had been killed.
- In 1935, marriage between black people and Aryans was banned in Germany.

JEWISH PERSECUTION

SOURCE R

Nazi scientists measuring noses to classify racial features. They believed that different races had different physical features.

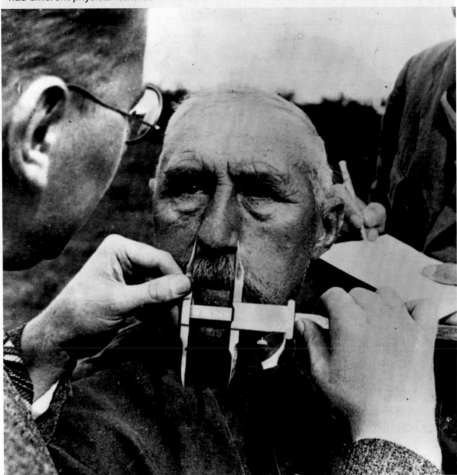

The Jews were a minority in Germany: around 1 per cent of Germany's population was Jewish. They had their own customs and their religion made them appear 'different'. After the First World War, many German people were keen to find a scapegoat. Hitler claimed the Jews were responsible for Germany's defeat in the war and the economic problems that followed.

Anti-Semitism was an established part of Nazi thinking; after Hitler took power, he was determined to take measures against the Jews. From 1933, life for Jews in Germany grew worse year by year.

- In April 1933, the Nazi government organised a nationwide **boycott** of Jewish shops and businesses. Stormtroopers stood outside Jewish shops to prevent people entering. In the same year, Jews were banned from government employment, medicine, teaching and journalism.
- In 1935, Jews were banned from public places, such as parks, cinemas and swimming pools. They were also banned from the army.
- In September 1935, the Nuremberg Laws were introduced. There were two of these laws. The Reich Law for the Protection of German Blood and Honour stated that Jews and Aryans could not marry. Aryans who were already married to Jews were encouraged to get a divorce; otherwise, they

KEY TERM

boycott when customers refuse to buy goods or services from certain people as a form of protest

would be treated in law as Jews. The Reich Law on **Citizenship** said only people of German blood were German citizens. Jews could no longer vote in elections or hold a German passport.

- Many Jews chose to emigrate to avoid **persecution**. In January 1939, the Reich Office for Jewish Emigration was set up and was responsible for speeding up the emigration of Jews. The Nazis banned **emigration** in 1941 but, by this time, almost two-thirds of German Jews had fled the country. The remaining 160,000 were unable to leave. They suffered a terrible fate when the Nazis introduced the Final Solution in 1942 (see page 96).

SOURCE S

A Jewish lawyer, wearing cut-off trousers, forced to walk without shoes through a German city. He has been made to wear a sign around his neck, which reads: 'I will never ever again file a complaint with the police'.

SOURCE T

From the website of the United States Holocaust Memorial Museum.

Many German… Jews tried to go to the United States but could not obtain the visas needed to enter… Many Americans believed that refugees would compete with them for jobs… In the summer of 1938, delegates from thirty-two countries met at the French resort of Evian… Delegate after delegate rose to express sympathy for the refugees. But most countries, including the United States and Britain, offered excuses for not letting in more refugees. The German government was able to state with great pleasure how 'astounding' it was that foreign countries criticized Germany for its treatment of the Jews, but none of them wanted to open the doors to them… Even efforts by some Americans to rescue children failed: the Wagner-Rogers bill, an effort to admit 20,000 endangered Jewish refugee children, was not supported by the Senate in 1939 and 1940.

From 1938, the situation for Jews got worse.

- All possessions had to be registered with the government. This meant that the Nazis knew exactly what people owned and could take whatever they wanted from the Jews.
- Jews were made to carry identity cards at all times; they had to present these cards when told to by any Nazi official.
- Jewish professionals, including doctors and lawyers, were not allowed to take on work for non-Jews.

THE NIGHT OF BROKEN GLASS – *KRISTALLNACHT*

In November 1938, a German official in the Paris Embassy was murdered by a Jewish man. This gave the Nazis an excuse to launch a campaign of terror and murder aimed at Jews in Germany. On the night of 9–10 November:

- over 800 shops owned by Jews were destroyed
- 191 **synagogues** were vandalised or set on fire
- many Jewish homes were attacked and property was damaged or stolen
- 91 Jews were killed and 30,000 were arrested.

The Nazi newspapers presented the events as a spontaneous reaction by ordinary German citizens, showing their anger about the murder of the German official. In reality, Goebbels and other Nazis had planned the attacks, but they hoped they would be interpreted as a genuine sign of anger and hatred towards German Jews. The Nazis were disappointed to discover that much of the damaged property was rented from German landlords and not owned by the Jews. When they realised this, they fined the Jewish community 1 billion Reichsmarks to pay for the damage.

However, as you will see in the next chapter, things were to get much worse for Jews in Germany.

EXTEND YOUR KNOWLEDGE

KINDERTRANSPORT 1938–40

Kindertransport (Children's Transport) was a scheme in which the British government took in around 10,000 refugee children from Nazi-occupied Europe. It was agreed that the children would return to their families when the crisis was over. Parents were not allowed to accompany the children.

After arriving in Britain, children with sponsors went to meet their foster families. Children without sponsors were housed in a camp until individual families agreed to care for them or until hostels could be organised to care for larger groups of children.

After the war, most of the children became citizens of Great Britain, or emigrated to Israel, the USA, Canada or Australia. Most of the parents were victims of the Holocaust and the children never saw them again.

ACTIVITY

1 Describe two ways in which Jews were persecuted up to 1935.
2 Why did the persecution get worse over time? Write a paragraph to explain your answer.

EXAM-STYLE QUESTION

A01   **A02**

SKILLS PROBLEM SOLVING, REASONING, DECISION MAKING, ADAPTIVE LEARNING, INNOVATION

'The impact of the Nuremberg Laws was the main reason life was difficult for German Jews in 1929–39.'

How far do you agree? Explain your answer.

You may use the following in your answer:
■ the impact of the Nuremberg Laws
■ Hitler's ideas in *Mein Kampf*.
You **must** use other information of your own.   **(16 marks)**

HINT

Think about all the difficulties that the Jews faced in this period. What caused those difficulties? Was it a deliberate policy by the government or group, or was it something that just happened by chance. Can you show how the causes led to the life of German Jews being difficult?

4.4 NAZI POLICIES TO REDUCE UNEMPLOYMENT

LEARNING OUTCOMES

- Understand how the Germans tried to introduce self-sufficiency
- Understand measures to reduce unemployment
- Understand how government organisations were set up to encourage workers.

KEY TERM

self-sufficient when a country can produce all the materials and goods it needs within its own nation; the Germans called this policy autarky

The Nazis had come to power largely as a result of the problems created by the Great Depression. Hitler had promised to end Germany's economic problems, so he had to reduce unemployment quickly. Unfortunately, Germany's trade – like that of the rest of the world – was suffering as a result of the Depression. In addition, Germany lacked essential **raw materials**. Part of the Nazi economic plan was to make Germany **self-sufficient**, so it would not have to rely on other countries.

ECONOMIC PLANS

- The Nazis' first plan was introduced by the Minister of the Economy, Dr Hjalmar Schact. His 'New Plan' was designed to reduce imports and reduce unemployment. Schact was fortunate that his plan came at a time when world trade was beginning to improve. He made trade agreements with other countries to guarantee Germany's supply of raw materials. He also began projects to create work, such as road building. His plan was very successful and provided Hitler with the money he needed to rearm Germany.
- From 1936, Hermann Goering was made responsible for the 'Four Year Plan' to prepare Germany for war. This plan involved making Germany self-sufficient in terms of oil, steel and rubber – that is, making sure Germany had its own supplies of these materials, so that it could wage war without worrying about losing resources it needed. Scientists were set to work to find substitutes; for example, textiles made from pulped wood. The Nazis called this **autarky**. The Four Year Plan was accompanied by a propaganda campaign to persuade people to buy German products and eat only German food. However, Goering's plan had limited success. There were frequent food shortages and **rationing** had to be introduced. In 1939, Germany had to import one-third of its raw materials.
- Although the work of Schact and Goering did bring some successes, government spending was always more than its income. By 1939 the government had a debt of over 40 billion marks. Despite autarky Germany was still importing more than it exported. Although millions more people were back in work, the average consumption of basic foodstuffs like bread, meat, milk and eggs actually dropped between 1937 and 1939.

REDUCING UNEMPLOYMENT

How was this huge drop in unemployment achieved?

- The Nazis continued with policies first introduced by the Weimar Republic after the Wall Street Crash. They doubled spending on public works programmes, such as building *autobahns* (motorways) and the Olympic Stadium in Berlin. This created jobs for construction workers.
- Hitler began to adopt a more aggressive foreign policy and rearmament became increasingly important. Spending on arms increased from around 2 million Reichsmarks in 1933 to 17 million Reichsmarks in 1937. This investment created many new jobs, both in arms factories and in related

industries (for example, **coal mining**, iron ore extraction, and industries producing iron, steel and chemicals).

■ The work of Schact and Goering was very important in helping the Nazis keep their promise of putting Germany back to work. In 1933 unemployment was at 6 million. By 1939, it had been reduced to only half a million.

■ The expansion of the German army also created employment. The Treaty of Versailles had limited Germany's army to 100,000 men but by 1938 there were more than 900,000 men in the army.

■ The Nazis paid private companies to create jobs. One of their most well-known investments was in the car industry, where they helped to produce the famous Volkswagen (People's Car). The Nazis claimed that the car would be cheaply available to all Germans, but most people did not get a chance to buy one until after the war, because the factory started making weapons instead.

ACTIVITY

Does Figure 4.7 show that Nazi economic policies were successful? Explain your answer.

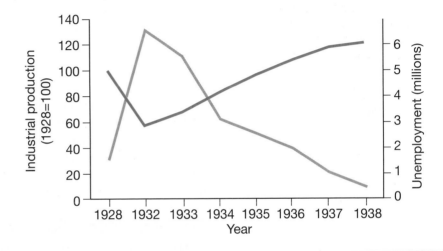

▶ **Figure 4.7** Industrial output (red) and unemployment (grey) in Nazi Germany

THE REALITY

The numbers in Figure 4.7 are very impressive, and suggest that the Nazis brought about a huge decrease in unemployment. However, they do not include what historians have called 'invisible unemployment'.

■ From 1933, women were encouraged to stay at home. Many of them gave up their jobs or were sacked. From 1937, women were encouraged back to work to support the rearmament programme. Despite this, fewer woman were working in 1939 than in 1929 (before the Depression). Women were not included in the Nazis' unemployment figures.

■ Jews were forced from their jobs and their positions were taken by Aryans. Jews were no longer considered citizens, so they were not counted in the unemployment figures.

■ The National Labour Service (RAD) was set up to organise unemployed men to do manual work. Single men had to serve 6 months in this service, because Hitler believed this would instil discipline and the value of hard physical work. After 1935, unemployed men were forced to join the RAD, and were no longer counted as unemployed. RAD workers were used to build the *autobahns* and other public building projects. Their work helped to create the impression that Nazi Germany was strong and advanced.

■ Anyone who had temporary employment, such as agricultural workers, was counted as being in full employment. As a result of these measures, over 1 million people who may have wanted work were excluded from the unemployment figures.

■ In addition, the statistics do not tell us what life was like for many Germans who were employed in this period. During the 1930s, there was an increase in wages but the number of hours worked per week also rose by close to 10 per cent. The cost of living rose as well, so the average worker's pay bought less in 1939 than it had done in 1933.

THE GERMAN LABOUR FRONT (DAF)

After the Nazis banned the trade unions, they set up a Nazi organisation called the German Labour Front, led by Dr Robert Ley. This was not a trade union – unions were seen as a threat, because they argued for improved workers' rights and were associated with communism. Instead, it was intended to ensure the efficient running of industry.

Both employers and employees were in the DAF. However, it soon became apparent that the main aims of the DAF were to get workers to work harder and to control wages. The DAF wanted more work without more pay, so it ran two programmes to try to improve workers' lives in other ways. These were 'Strength Through Joy' and the 'Beauty of Labour'.

STRENGTH THROUGH JOY (KDF)

The purpose of this scheme was to run activities for workers in their leisure time. The intention was to create satisfied workers who would then work harder and be more productive at work. Rewards were offered for the hardest workers – for example, subsidised cruises and holidays, cheap tickets at the theatre, sports competitions or free courses at the German Adult Education Office. Very few people were able to go on a cruise, however; museum tours were much more common. Strength Through Joy was also responsible for the Volkswagen project.

SOURCE U

Strength through Joy. Volkswagens being presented to the public outside the town hall in Berlin in 1939.

BEAUTY OF LABOUR (SDA)

This part of the DAF was responsible for improving working conditions. It encouraged employers to provide canteens serving hot meals, and sport and leisure facilities. Many employers did provide these facilities, but they often expected the workers to build them in their spare time and took contributions towards their running costs from employees' wages.

RECAP

RECALL QUIZ

1   What was the name of the Nazi secret police?
2   In which year was the Enabling Act passed?
3   Who was the head of the Ministry of Propaganda?
4   What was the name of the law that forbade marriage between Jews and Aryans?
5   Who was made to swear an oath of allegiance (loyalty) to Hitler from August 1934?
6   What was the name of the Nazi youth group that girls were expected to join?
7   What organisation was set up to control the Protestant church?
8   What does the term *Kristallnacht* mean?
9   What was the name of the Nazi workers' organisation that replaced the trade unions?
10 What was autarky?

CHECKPOINT

STRENGTHEN

S1 Name three methods that the Nazis used to control information in Germany.
S2 In what ways did the Nazis try to control the power and influence of the Church in Germany?
S3 In what ways was Nazi education similar and different for boys and girls?

CHALLENGE

C1 How far did the role of women change under the Nazi government, compared with the situation under the Weimar Republic?
C2 How was the Reichstag important in helping Hitler to destroy German democracy?
C3 How important was Goebbels in ensuring Nazi control over the people of Germany?

SUMMARY

- The Reichstag fire gave Hitler the opportunity to start building a dictatorship in Germany.
- The Enabling Act changed Germany's constitution. It gave much more power to Hitler.
- The Night of the Long Knives, which saw SA leaders killed, enabled Hitler to strengthen his control of the Nazi Party.
- After Hindenburg's death, Hitler declared himself Führer.
- Nazi Germany was a police state.
- Religion was closely controlled and the Nazis introduced measures to weaken the influence of the Church in Germany.
- In Nazi Germany, censorship and propaganda were used to control and influence attitudes.
- Young people were controlled in school and outside school through Nazi youth groups.
- Women were expected to focus on 'children, church and kitchen'.
- Jews were persecuted with increasing severity in the period from 1933–39.
- Measures were taken to introduce economic self-sufficiency and reduce unemployment.

EXAM GUIDANCE: PART (C) QUESTIONS

A01   **A02**

SKILLS PROBLEM SOLVING, REASONING, DECISION MAKING, ADAPTIVE LEARNING, INNOVATION

Question to be answered: 'The greatest change in the lives of people in Germany in the years 1933–39 was the reduction in unemployment.'

How far do you agree? Explain your answer.

You may use the following in your answer:
- **the reduction in unemployment**
- **the school curriculum.**

You must also use information of your own.   (16 marks)

1 **Analysis Question 1: What is the question type testing?**
In this question, you have to demonstrate that you have knowledge and understanding of the key features and characteristics of the period studied. You also have to analyse historical events and periods so you can explain and make judgements about the role of various factors in causing something to happen. In this case, you must consider how life changed in Germany under the Nazis.

2 **Analysis Question 2: What do I have to do to answer the question well?**
- You have been given two factors to write about – the reduction in unemployment and the school curriculum. You don't have to use the stimulus material provided, but you will find it difficult to assess the impact of the reduction in unemployment if you don't write about it!
- The question also says that you must include information of your own. This means that you need to include at least one other factor, as well as the two you have been given. For example, you could talk about censorship and how this affected people's lives.
- Make sure you do not simply give information. Think about how the factors you write about brought changes to people's lives.
- The question asks whether the reduction in unemployment was the main change, so you must compare the changes you write about and make a judgement about which one was most significant.

3 **Analysis Question 3: Are there any techniques I can use to make it very clear that I am doing what is needed to be successful?**
This is a 16-mark question so you need to make sure you give a substantial answer. You will be up against time pressures so try using these techniques to help you succeed.
- Only give a brief introduction, which answers the question straight away and shows what your paragraphs are going to be about.
- Try to use the words of the question at the beginning of each paragraph. This will help you to stay focused and avoid writing narrative.
- Remember this question is about changes. Make sure your answer explains how things changed (or didn't change).
- Don't simply state which change was greatest. Make sure you explain your choice by comparing the different changes.

In summary, to score high marks on this question, you need to do three things:
- provide coverage of content range (at least three changes)
- provide coverage of arguments for and against the statement in the question
- provide clear reasons (criteria) for an overall judgement, backed by convincing argument.

Answer

Here is a student response to the question. The teacher has made some comments.

A good concise introduction, identifying three factors. However, I'm not sure it's a valid argument to say that the reduction in unemployment was the main change because people were worried about their jobs.

I think the reduction in unemployment was the main change, because people were very worried about jobs. However, the changes in the school curriculum were significant, and so were the changes to the lives of Jewish people.

This is relevant information and well expressed, but it is purely descriptive. How was this a change and how important was it?

When Hitler came to power, 6 million Germans were unemployed. One of the reasons that the Nazis had come to power was because the Weimar Republic had not been able to cope with the Wall Street Crash. The Nazis reduced unemployment to only half a million by 1939. They did this in a number of ways. They had a huge public works programme which involved building things such as autobahns and the Olympic stadium in Berlin. As the economy grew, more and more people were involved in coal mining and in the armaments factories. Hitler's aggressive foreign policy needed a bigger army, so almost 1 million men ended up in the armed forces.

Again, this is good detail – although the Hitler Youth is irrelevant because it isn't part of the school curriculum. However, you haven't talked about how much of this is a change and how important it was.

There was a lot of change in the school curriculum. New subjects, such as 'Race Studies' were brought in and PE became a central part of the curriculum, so boys would be fit for the army and girls would be fit for motherhood. The Nazis used the school curriculum to promote their views, so Biology taught about the supremacy of the Aryan race and History taught about the great history of the Nazis. The Nazis also set up the Hitler Youth where boys and girls were indoctrinated with Nazi views on the supremacy of the Aryan race and the importance of a strong military.

Same again! Good information but no explanation.

In September 1935, the Nuremberg Laws were introduced. These said that Jews and Aryans could not marry and that, unless they divorced, Aryans who were married to Jews would be treated as Jews from now on. Jews were no longer allowed to vote or hold a German passport. From 1938, Jews had to register their possessions with the government and carry an identity card showing that they were Jewish. Jewish doctors and lawyers could only work for Jewish clients. Then, in November 1938, 91 Jews were killed on Kristallnacht, when shops and synagogues were attacked.

A disappointing conclusion; you haven't stated which change was most significant. You should use your conclusion to draw together the points in your answer and make a judgement.

In conclusion, they were all very important.

What are the strengths and weaknesses of this answer?
You can see the strengths and weaknesses of this answer from what the teacher says. There is quite a bit of relevant information here, but there is a lack of explanation. A lot of this answer is just narrative – 'telling the story'.

Work with a friend
Discuss with a friend how you would rewrite the weaker paragraphs in the answer to enable the whole answer to get high marks. Then work out what you ought to put in the conclusion.

Does your answer do the following things?

Answer checklist
☐ Identify changes
☐ Provide detailed information to show how change occurred
☐ Provide at least one factor other than those given in the question
☐ Identify the 'main change' by looking at arguments for and against and comparing them.

Doing it differently

The answer above has looked at the two stimulus factors given – reduction in unemployment and the school curriculum – and also considered the changes to the lives of Jews. However, there are many other factors that you could have considered.

Here is a list of some alternative factors you could use to show how life changed under the Nazis. For each factor, the start of the paragraph is given. Work with a friend to write the rest of each paragraph, explaining the changes.

- One area where there was a considerable change in people's lives was religion. Hitler had strong views on the Churches and was determined to bring them under control.
- The position of women in Nazi Germany was very interesting. In some ways, their lives changed significantly, but in other ways they were encouraged to take a very traditional role in society.
- There was much less freedom under the Nazis in terms of what newspapers were allowed to print, what was said on the radio – even the music people listened to, the art they looked at, and the books they read. Censorship was everywhere.
- Although Nazi measures reduced unemployment, life didn't necessarily improve for workers. For many workers, things actually got worse.

Summing it up

- Can you think of any factors which have not been covered?
- Look at all the factors above and decide which one brought about the greatest change. Now write a conclusion which would finish your essay, explaining why this factor was more important than the others.

5. GERMANY AND THE OCCUPIED TERRITORIES DURING THE SECOND WORLD WAR

LEARNING OBJECTIVES

- Understand the impact of Nazi policies towards the Jews in the Second World War
- Understand the impact of the Second World War on German civilians
- Understand the growth of opposition to Hitler and the Nazis.

In 1939, Germany invaded Poland and Europe was at war. During the first 2 years of the war, Germany took control of much of Central and Western Europe. Large numbers of Jews lived in these territories. At first, the Germans herded the Jews into ghettos in the poorer parts of cities. From January 1942, they began a new policy. Existing concentration camps were converted into extermination camps and 6 million Jews were killed in these camps. This became known as the Holocaust.

The Second World War had a significant impact on the life of civilians in Germany. In the early years of the war, rationing was only a minor problem. From 1942, as the Allies began to win the war, there were serious shortages of essential items. In addition, the Allies carried out bombing raids on German cities, which made life very unpleasant for the Germans.

The Nazis kept a tight control on the German people. However, as conditions in Germany grew worse, there was growing opposition – particularly among younger Germans. There was even an attempt to blow up Hitler in July 1944. Hitler survived the assassination attempt but his leadership of Germany was coming to an end as Germany faced defeat in the war. In April 1945, Hitler committed suicide. One week later, Germany surrendered.

5.1 NAZI POLICIES TOWARDS THE JEWS

LEARNING OBJECTIVES

- Understand the Nazi policy of ghettoisation
- Understand why the Nazis introduced the Final Solution
- Understand the impact of the Final Solution.

During the 1930s, life for Jews in Germany became increasingly difficult. Their civil rights were withdrawn one by one and thousands of them were sent to concentration camps. During the Second World War, the persecution of the Jews became worse. By 1942, the Nazi policy of persecution had changed to a policy of **genocide**.

> **KEY TERM**
>
> genocide the deliberate killing of people of a particular nation or ethnic group

During the Second World War, German forces took control of much of Europe. By the end of 1941, only Britain and the Soviet Union prevented Hitler from having total domination of Europe. By this time, following mass emigration in the 1930s, there were fewer than 200,000 Jews in Germany. As new territories were occupied, however, millions more Jews came under Nazi control. In Poland – which the Germans occupied in 1939 – there were 3 million Jews. The Germans could not remove all these people by emigration, so other approaches had to be used.

GHETTOS

> **KEY TERM**
>
> ghetto an area of a city or town restricted to one minority group

The Germans began a policy of **ghettoisation**. This meant that all the Jews were forced to move to **ghettos** in the cities in Poland; the Germans called these 'Jewish Quarters'. The ghettos were walled-off areas where Jews were crammed into poor housing. Food was restricted and starvation was common. Conditions were very crowded and diseases such as typhus spread rapidly. In Warsaw, the Jewish ghetto was surrounded by a 3.5 metre high wall, topped with barbed wire and broken glass. The wall was built by a German company, but the local Jewish community was forced to pay for its construction. Between January 1941 and July 1942, an average of almost 4,000 Jews died each month from disease and starvation.

In July 1942, after the introduction of the 'Final Solution' (see below), the Germans announced that the Warsaw Jews were to be 'resettled' in the east of Poland. Over 250,000 Jews were transported to camps in eastern Poland. Here, most of them were put to death.

EXAM-STYLE QUESTION

A01 **A02**

Explain **two** effects on Jews of the Nazi policy of setting up Jewish ghettos.

(8 marks)

> **HINT**
>
> You can include the effects that might not have happened until later.

An account of the suicide of Adam Czerniakow, chairman of the Jewish Council in Warsaw in July 1942.

Realising that the Germans intended to exterminate the Jews of Warsaw, Adam Czerniakow committed suicide. Before swallowing the tablet he wrote two notes, one to the Jewish Council executive and the other to his wife. In the first he said that the Germans had visited him that day and told him the expulsion order applied to children as well. They could not expect him to hand over helpless children for destruction. He had therefore decided to put an end to his life. He had asked his colleagues not to see this as an act of cowardice.

The German authorities announce the resettlement of Jews living in Warsaw in July 1942.

All Jews will be resettled to the east, regardless of age and sex, with the exception of:
- Jews working for German institutions or companies
- Jews working for the Jewish Council
- Jewish Hospital staff

Every resettled Jew will be allowed to bring 15kg of luggage and all valuables, gold jewellery, money etc.

Provisions for three days must be taken.

The resettlement will start on 22 July 1942 at 11 o'clock.

The Jewish Council is responsible for the delivery of 6,000 persons daily until 4 o'clock.

Assembly point is the Jewish Hospital which has to be emptied so that the building can be used for the people being resettled.

The Jewish Council has to announce the German orders to the Jewish people.

Punishments
- Any Jew who leaves the ghetto during the resettlement action will be shot
- Any Jew who acts against the resettlement will be shot

ACTIVITY

1 Why do you think the Germans forced the Jews to live in ghettos?
2 Read Source A. Are there any parts of the German announcement which you find surprising? If so, which ones?
3 What can you learn about the Final Solution from Source B?

DEATH SQUADS

In June 1941, the Germans invaded the Soviet Union. They quickly conquered most of the west of the country, and thousands more Jews came under Nazi control. Special units, known as *Einsatzgruppen*, followed the German army; they had orders to put Jews to death. These death squads rounded up all Jewish men, women and children (as well as Communist Party leaders and gypsies) and confiscated any valuables they owned. The victims were then forced to remove their clothing and march to fields and forests on the outskirts of towns. Here, the Jews were shot or **gassed** and their bodies were thrown into mass graves. It is thought that the *Einsatzgruppen* had murdered over 1.2 million civilians in the Soviet Union by 1943.

EXTEND YOUR KNOWLEDGE

Ejszyszki is a small town in what is now Lithuania. On 21 September 1941, a mobile killing squad entered the town. They herded 4,000 Jewish men, women and children from the town and the surrounding region into three synagogues. The Jews were held here for 2 days without food or water. Then, they were taken to cemeteries, lined up in front of open pits, and shot. Today there are no Jews in Ejszyszki.

THE FINAL SOLUTION

In July 1941, the Nazis came up with a plan – a 'Final Solution' to the Jewish problem. Concentration camps were built in eastern Poland and Jews were sent to these camps to carry out forced labour. At a conference in Wannsee in Berlin in January 1942, the Nazis decided to convert some of these concentration camps into **extermination** camps where Jews would be killed. Over the next 4 years, almost 6 million Jews were put to death; this has become known as the **Holocaust**. Historians believe that another 5 million non-Jews (including gypsies, homosexuals, priests and people with disabilities) also died in camps such as Auschwitz, Treblinka and Sobibor.

KEY TERM

Holocaust destruction or slaughter on a large scale; here it refers to the slaughter of the Jews

Jews sent to the camps were divided into two groups. People who were fit enough to work were given jobs to do until they were too weak to perform them. Some of these people were forced to take part in medical experiments – to see, for example, how long a human could survive in extreme cold, or to find out the effect on one twin if the other twin was infected with a deadly disease.

The rest were killed. The extermination of so many people was a huge task and shooting proved to be too slow, so the Germans decided to use poison gas instead. Huge showers were built and up to 2,000 Jews at a time were sent into these showers, supposedly for 'delousing' (the removal of lice). Poison gas was then released into the chambers. After all the victims were dead, other prisoners removed the bodies. Any useful 'by-products' – such as gold teeth, hair and glasses – were removed and the bodies were then transported to huge ovens to be burned.

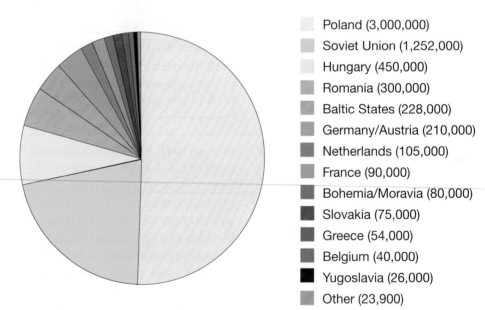

Poland (3,000,000)
Soviet Union (1,252,000)
Hungary (450,000)
Romania (300,000)
Baltic States (228,000)
Germany/Austria (210,000)
Netherlands (105,000)
France (90,000)
Bohemia/Moravia (80,000)
Slovakia (75,000)
Greece (54,000)
Belgium (40,000)
Yugoslavia (26,000)
Other (23,900)

▶ **Figure 5.1** The number of Jews killed in death camps and by death squads. ('Other' includes Bulgaria: 14,000; Italy: 8,000; Luxembourg: 1,000; and Norway: 900.)

KEEPING IT SECRET

The round-up of Jews was a massive task and would have been extremely difficult if people had known what was happening in the camps. To ensure the process went smoothly, propaganda films were made showing that the resettlement camps were no more than labour camps. The videos showed that the people were treated well and lived in good conditions. This stopped the German people from reacting negatively to what was happening. It also meant that Jewish people were willing to help organise the resettlement of fellow Jews.

ACTIVITY

1 Why do you think the Germans made propaganda films showing good conditions in resettlement camps?

2 Why did the Jews in the Warsaw ghetto not believe that conditions in the camps were good?

3 'Maximilian Kolbe's decision to volunteer to take the place of another prisoner at Auschwitz was pointless because they were all going to die anyway.' Discuss with a partner whether you agree with this comment.

Over time, however, the Jews came to realise what was happening. In April 1943, there was an uprising in the Warsaw ghetto against transportation to the camps. After a month of fighting, the remaining 56,000 Jews were arrested: 7,000 of them were shot and the rest were sent to the camps.

When it became clear that Germany was losing the war, the Nazis tried to hide what had happened by digging up the railway lines and destroying some records. Allied soldiers were shocked by the reality when the camps were liberated in 1945. Rudolph Hoess, the commandant of Auschwitz camp, was hanged for war crimes at Auschwitz in 1947.

EXTEND YOUR KNOWLEDGE

MAXIMILIAN KOLBE

Maximilian Kolbe was a Catholic priest who ran a hospital at his Polish monastery. This hospital hid up to 3,000 Polish refugees, many of them Jews. In 1941, Kolbe's monastery was shut down and he was arrested and transferred to Auschwitz. While Kolbe was in Auschwitz, three prisoners vanished from the camp. The enraged guards decided to starve ten men to death to deter further escapees. One of the chosen men pleaded that he had a wife and children, so Kolbe volunteered to take his place. Kolbe was the last of the ten left alive and he was finally executed by lethal injection. He was later made a saint, and there is a statue of him over the door of London's Westminster Abbey.

SOURCE C

Survivors in a liberated concentration camp in 1945.

EXTRACT A

An extract from a history of Germany, written in 2009.

In the summer of 1941, a decision was taken by senior Nazi leaders to seek a permanent and final solution to the Jewish question. It was to exterminate them in death camps… Death camps were built in Poland, far away from Germany, where Jews were to be worked to death… By the summer of 1943, Jews from all over Europe were being transported to these camps… On arrival at the death camps, the Jews were divided into two groups. Those who were fit were put to work. The others were sent to the gas chambers.

EXAM-STYLE QUESTION

A04

SKILLS ANALYSIS, INTERPRETATION, CREATIVITY

Study Extract A.

What impression does the author give about the treatment of the Jews?

You **must** use Extract A to explain your answer.   **(6 marks)**

HINT

Make sure you quote extensively from the extract to support your answer.

5.2 THE HOME FRONT DURING THE WAR

LEARNING OBJECTIVES

☐ Understand the impact of the war on German civilians, especially women

☐ Understand the impact of 'total war'

☐ Understand the impact of Allied bombing.

Although there was great support for Hitler's aggressive foreign policy, when it became clear that Britain was not going to be defeated quickly, enthusiasm for the war declined. As shortages and rationing began to bite, a sense of disillusionment set in among the German people.

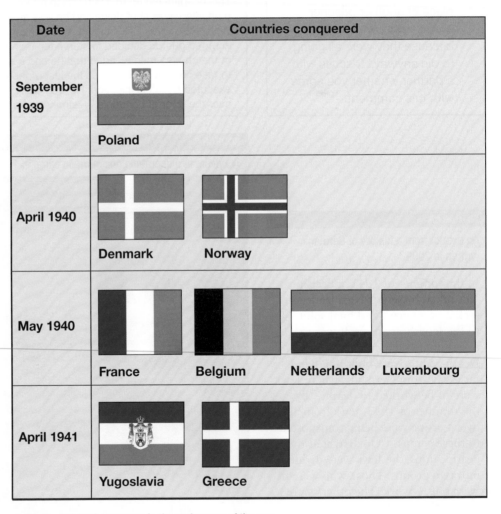

Date	Countries conquered
September 1939	Poland
April 1940	Denmark Norway
May 1940	France Belgium Netherlands Luxembourg
April 1941	Yugoslavia Greece

▲ **Figure 5.2** Nazi conquests in the early years of the war

EVACUATION

As in Britain, the Germans made plans at the start of the war to **evacuate** children from major centres of population, such as Berlin. At first, many families chose not to send their children away. But as Allied bombing attacks became more common from 1942, mass evacuation began with children being sent into rural areas, such as Bavaria. About 2.5 million German children were evacuated into rural areas as part of the *Kinderlandverschickung* (KLV) programme. Unlike in Britain, those children did not stay in individual homes, but instead were placed in one of 9,000 camps supervised by Hitler Youth leaders and teachers.

RATIONING

The first rationing began in August 1939 and included bread, meat, dairy products, soap and, from November, clothing. Food stamps were issued to civilians and the appropriate number of stamps had to be handed over when food was bought. Soldiers on home leave were also issued food stamps. Theft of stamps was a criminal offence and typically resulted in a sentence at a forced labour camp.

If you ate at a restaurant, you not only had to pay for the meal, but you also had to provide enough stamps to cover the food you had eaten. The rations were sufficient for people to maintain a basic level of nutrition, but there were many shortages, and some things were very difficult to find. Toilet paper was almost non-existent, tobacco was so rare that it could be used to buy other goods, and shortages of coal and shoes in the winters of 1939–40 and 1940–41 made people very unhappy.

In the early part of the war, goods were shipped back from occupied countries to help solve the problems of shortages, but as the war continued there were so many shortages that in May 1942 the government cut rations. Bread was restricted to about half a loaf per person per day, and meat to just 40 grams per day. Of course, anything you wanted could be bought on the black market, but at a hugely inflated price.

The German people learned to cope with food shortages. However, towards the end of the war, over 3 million Germans living in the east of the country fled west to escape from the advancing Soviet army. They found many cities destroyed by Allied bombing and a serious shortage of food. Their arrival added to the problem, and in some areas there was starvation in the last months of the war.

TOTAL WAR

KEY TERM

scorched earth policy a military strategy of burning or destroying crops or other resources that might be useful to an invading enemy force

In June 1941, Hitler launched Operation Barbarossa – the invasion of the Soviet Union. At first, the Germans advanced rapidly and by November they were threatening Moscow, Leningrad and Kiev. In late November, however, temperatures dropped sharply and the German advance came to a halt. The soldiers were short of both winter equipment and supplies. The Soviet forces had adopted a **scorched earth policy** as they had retreated, destroying anything that might have been useful to the Germans. As a result, the Germans found themselves caught in a prolonged and fierce battle, in which over 2 million German soldiers are thought to have died.

SOURCE D

An extract from the diary of Joseph Goebbels in July 1941. Before the German invasion of the Soviet Union, the two countries had been allies since 1939, when they had signed an agreement to split Poland between them.

The Führer thinks that the action will take only 4 months; I think – even less. Communism will collapse as a house of cards. We are facing an unprecedented victorious campaign.

Cooperation with Russia was in fact a stain on our reputation. Now it is going to be washed out. The very thing we were struggling against for our whole lives, will now be destroyed. I tell this to the Führer and he agrees with me completely.

ACTIVITY

1 Why do you think Hitler invaded the Soviet Union?
2 Explain the meaning of the cartoon in Source E.

SOURCE E

A Soviet cartoon showing Hitler ordering his troops to invade the Soviet Union.

The failures in the Soviet Union, and defeats elsewhere in the war, placed Germany under great strain. Until the failure of Operation Barbarossa it was expected that the war would be over in just a few years. But in February 1943 Goebbels told the German people that they were now involved in 'total war'. All of Germany's resources and all of its people had to be fully committed to fighting for victory. Everything had to be used for winning the war.

One of the problems Germany faced in fighting such a war was a growing shortage of labour to work in the factories. Various measures were taken to try to deal with this shortage.

■ In the early years of the war, workers were recruited from the occupied countries. In October 1941, Hitler announced that Russian prisoners of war could be transported to Germany to act as slave labour. By 1944, over 7 million prisoners were working for German industry.

EXTEND YOUR KNOWLEDGE

THEY CLOSED THE SWEET SHOPS!
When the Germans closed small businesses during the war, there were some unintended consequences. Some people in Hanover complained that the sweet shops had been closed, even though many of these shops were run by elderly women who could certainly not transfer to war work. So, there was a shortage of sweets.

- From January 1943, all men aged 16–65 and all women aged 17–45 had to register as available for work. Small businesses which were not essential for the war effort were closed and their employees were taken into the army or transferred to war work. However, there were many exemptions to the rules about women registering for work, because Hitler did not approve of married women working.
- In August 1944 a ban on holidays for workers was introduced and the working week was increased to 60 hours.
- By 1943 the labour shortage was so serious that Hitler had to allow women to help the war effort.

Other measures were taken to help fight Germany's 'total war'. For example:
- professional sports teams and places of entertainment were shut down (although cinemas were kept open)
- postal services were reduced to save fuel
- the *Volkssturm* (Home Guard) was formed to help protect Germany from any invasion. By the end of the war, boys as young as 12 were being forced to join the *Volkssturm*.

EXAM-STYLE QUESTION

A01 **A02**

SKILLS PROBLEM SOLVING, REASONING, DECISION MAKING, ADAPTIVE LEARNING, INNOVATION

'Rationing was the most important impact on the German people of the Second World War.'

How far do you agree? Explain your answer.

You may use the following in your answer:
- rationing
- war work.

You **must** also use information of your own.   **(16 marks)**

> **HINT**
>
> Note that the question says you must use information of your own. Consider other aspects of the Second World War. Was there a change in the way Jews were treated, for example?

THE EFFECTS OF ALLIED BOMBING

From August 1940 the British RAF carried out bombing attacks on German cities. At first they bombed military and industrial targets, but the impact on German production was minimal. From 1942 a new tactic was used. The British and Americans began bombing civilian areas in an attempt to destroy German morale. Between March and July 1943 43 German cities were bombed, causing severe damage. The raids on Hamburg in the summer of 1943 killed 42,600 German civilians and forced around 1 million others to flee the city.

The government tried to reduce the impact of the bombing of German cities with stories of bravery and determination. It also set up welfare organisations to provide food and drink, and to help find accommodation for those people whose homes had been destroyed. Despite what the German propaganda said, the bombing certainly had a negative impact on the morale of the German people. However, as happened during the Blitz in Britain, it is also true that most people just tried to carry on with their normal lives – and to turn up at work as usual – despite the difficulties.

From 1944 the Allies began to focus once more on strategic targets such as railway lines, bridges and motorways, but a British survey in 1944 estimated that the bombing raids reduced German war production by only about 1 per cent. However, some industries suffered significant setbacks as a result of the bombing. Allied raids on the Ruhr Valley in 1944 are thought to have reduced metal production by around 40 per cent. It is also true that, while the bombing may have had a limited impact on war production, it did affect the transport of war goods. For example, in 1945 the Allies found several hundred tanks at a railway yard in Munich. Allied bombing had destroyed the railway line and made it impossible to send the tanks to the front.

EXAM-STYLE QUESTION

A01 A02

Explain **two** effects on the German people of Allied bombing from 1943.

(8 marks)

HINT

Do not explain why the Allies bombed Germany – or even how. Limit your answer to what the effects were – that means what the impact was.

EXTEND YOUR KNOWLEDGE

VICTIMS OF THE BOMBING

Over 600,000 Germans died as a result of Allied bombing, including 76,000 children. Many of the deaths came as people sheltered in cellars to avoid being killed or injured by the falling bombs. Unfortunately for them, the firestorms created by the bombs sucked all the oxygen out of the cellars, so the sheltering Germans could not breathe. This explains why some Germans who seemed perfectly healthy collapsed in the street and died.

ACTIVITY

1 What is meant by 'total war'?
2 Make a list of the three worst impacts of the Second World War on the civilian population of Germany. Compare your list with others in your class. Do you all agree?

SOURCE F

The German city of Hamburg after the 1943 bombing raids. Hamburg was bombed seven times in the summer of 1943.

THE CHANGING ROLE OF WOMEN

As you read in Chapter 4, Hitler strongly believed that a woman's place was in the home raising children. The Nazi government encouraged working women to leave paid employment and devote their time to looking after their families. Although some women had to return to work in 1936 to support the rearmament programme, there were fewer women working in 1939 than there had been in 1929.

During the war, many men left work to join the armed forces and there was a shortage of workers in the factories. The government now had the power to conscript women to work in factories, but Hitler's opposition to women working meant that the number of female workers in industry actually dropped between 1939 and 1941.

As the war continued, however, industry could not do without women workers. In June 1941 Goering ordered that any woman who had previously been in paid employment and had no children should register for work. When the policy of 'total war' was introduced in 1943, all women aged 17–45 had to register and by mid-1943 half a million extra women were working in industry. Even so, in November 1943, Hitler turned down a request to raise the age limit to 50, though he had to agree to this in 1945. By the end of the war women made up 60 per cent of Germany's labour force. Women also played a role as auxiliaries (assistants) in the armed forces where they operated searchlights and anti-aircraft guns.

It is important to also remember the psychological impact of the war on women. Many of them lived in constant fear of hearing that husbands or sons had been killed in the fighting, others struggled to raise their family with the father away and German cities suffering from heavy bombing and food shortages. Many women were killed in air raids, many were made homeless, and many were forced to leave their homes to move to safer areas. As the war came to an end the women also had to cope with the fear that the Soviet army was nearing Germany. Nazi propaganda had led the Germans to believe that the Soviets would treat women brutally. We know that Soviet soldiers did rape millions of German women in East Prussia and Berlin and that tens of thousands of women died from the attacks or committed suicide to avoid being attacked.

5.3 THE GROWTH OF OPPOSITION TO HITLER

LEARNING OBJECTIVES

- Understand the nature of German society during the Second World War
- Understand how and why opposition to the Nazis grew
- Understand the nature of opposition to the Nazis.

SOURCE G

A joke told in Nazi Germany.

The Führer visits a lunatic asylum and all the patients make the Nazi salute. Then Hitler notices one man not saluting. 'Why do you not greet me in the same way as everyone else?', Hitler asks. 'Ah', says the man. 'I work here, I am not a lunatic.'

During the 1930s, any opposition to Nazi rule had been dealt with severely. Other political parties were banned, trade union leaders were arrested, the media was censored and the Churches were brought under control. German children were forced to accept 'correct' (Nazi) ideas by the Hitler Youth and the Nazi control of education, and the SS and Gestapo punished anyone who did not conform.

Despite these measures, there was still some opposition to the Nazis. Some of this was organised, such as the communist **resistance** movement which operated underground. Most, however, was just the day-to-day grumbling which exists in any society. This was often in the form of anti-Nazi jokes (see Source G and Extract A) – though it would have been very dangerous to make these jokes in public.

EXTRACT A

From an article in an American newspaper in 2012.

Political jokes were not a form of resistance. They were a release valve for pent-up popular anger. People told jokes… because they coveted a moment of liberation in which they could let off a bit of steam. [The Nazis] rarely cracked down on joke-tellers and if they did, the punishments were mild – mostly resulting in a small fine. In the last phase of the war when the regime felt threatened by 'dissenters', though, this changed. A handful of death sentences were handed down to joke-tellers…

The long-term opponents of the Nazis were the German Communist Party. Following the German invasion of the Soviet Union, the party stepped up its secret campaigning against the government and is believed to have set up more than 100 underground cells across Germany. However, the Gestapo managed to infiltrate the party and it was never really a major threat to the Nazis.

As you saw in Chapter 4, there was opposition from within the Church. Although the Roman Catholic Church supported the German invasion of the Soviet Union, individual priests spoke out against the Nazis policies towards those with mental or physical disabilities. Members of the Protestant Confessional Church read a statement in the churches in 1943 criticising the treatment of Jews. Although Hitler was reluctant to take measures against priests and pastors, a number were executed for opposing the Nazi regime.

Among the most powerful and influential members of German society, there was also some opposition to the Nazi regime. A group called the Kreisau Circle met a number of times in 1942/3 to discuss how to oppose Nazism. The members of the group included German nobility, lawyers and politicians who did not like the way that Nazism crushed personal freedoms. However, the Gestapo found out about the group and broke it up.

As the Second World War began to have a greater impact on the everyday life of ordinary Germans, there was a definite increase in opposition to Nazi rule. As the Allied advance began to reach major German cities, there was increasing sabotage of the defence measures that German cities put in place to resist the advance. Many Germans had lost the will to resist and just wanted the war to end. But unlike when the First World War ended, there was no uprising against the government. Most Germans carried on being loyal to government until Germany was defeated.

Opposition to the Nazis was most visible among young people. Although the Hitler Youth movement was popular with many young Germans, there were others who did not agree with the military nature of the movement. They wanted greater freedom – for example, to form their own views, to dress how they liked and to listen to 'non-Nazi approved' music.

THE SWING YOUTH

Members of the Swing Youth were generally middle-class Germans who wanted to listen to American and British 'swing' music. They particularly liked jazz, which the Nazis considered 'degenerate' because of its links to black Americans. Swing Youth groups started in many major German towns and the Nazis took steps to stamp them out. Some leading members of the movement were arrested and served short sentences in concentration camps.

THE EDELWEISS PIRATES

The Edelweiss Pirate movement started in the Rhineland in 1937, before spreading to other areas of Germany. Members hated the Hitler Youth and frequently bullied or beat up its members. The Edelweiss Pirates objected to conscription and the training for military service which the Hitler Youth involved. Members were mainly working class and strongly **anti-establishment**; they continually found ways to criticise Nazi culture, and their dress and musical tastes did not follow Nazi fashion. They were also suspected of producing the anti-Nazi and anti-war **graffiti** that appeared in some German towns.

The Pirates were never really a threat to the Nazis. However, their activities did become more serious as the war progressed. For example:

- they gave shelter to army deserters and escaped prisoners from concentration camps
- they stole food and supplies from stores or freight trains
- they derailed train cars full of ammunition and supplied adult resistance groups with explosives
- in 1944, Barthel Schink (a member of the Cologne Pirates) was executed for planning to blow up a Gestapo building in Cologne.

THE WHITE ROSE GROUP

This group was founded by Hans and Sophie Scholl. Most members were students at Munich University. The group criticised the treatment of the Jews and Slavs and campaigned against the continuation of the war. In 1942–43, the group published six leaflets criticising the Nazis. In one leaflet, they wrote that Hitler was leading Germany to inevitable defeat. If the German people didn't stand up to him, at the end of the war they would be labelled barbarians in the same way that the Nazis were. They then painted anti-Nazi messages on buildings in Munich. Eventually, the Scholls were caught and executed.

EXTEND YOUR KNOWLEDGE

HANS AND SOPHIE SCHOLL

Sophie Scholl was so frightened about what the White Rose Group was doing that she slept in her brother's bed. On 18 February 1943, she and her brother went to Munich University to distribute anti-Nazi leaflets. Sophie had a few left over so she threw them over a balcony to float down to the students below. She was seen by a worker, who called the Gestapo. Hans Scholl had a draft for another leaflet in his pocket. He tried to swallow it, but the Gestapo were too quick. On 22 February 1943, just 4 days after being arrested, the Scholls were found guilty of treason and executed by guillotine. Hans Scholl's last words before he was executed were 'Long live freedom!'

SOURCE H

A postage stamp issued in Germany in 1961.

ACTIVITY

'The members of the youth groups who opposed the government were just silly young people who were never a threat to Nazi rule'. Write a 30 second speech to convince your classmates that this statement is either correct or incorrect.

THE JULY BOMB PLOT (1944)

Hitler had almost fanatical support from the German military but some army leaders opposed his brutal methods and anti-Semitic policies. As Germany began to lose the war – particularly after the failings in the Soviet Union – these leaders decided to act. The group was led by General Ludwig Beck, Colonel Claus von Stauffenberg and the anti-Nazi politician, Dr Carl Goerdeler. The plan was that Goerdeler would be chancellor once Hitler had been killed.

On 20 July 1944, von Stauffenberg took a bomb in a briefcase into a meeting at Hitler's military headquarters in East Prussia. He then said he had an urgent phone call to make and left the meeting. Unfortunately, after von Stauffenberg had left, one of the other army leaders moved his briefcase. Four people were killed when the bomb went off, but Hitler survived.

Von Stauffenberg and Beck tried to seize control of Berlin but, with Hitler still alive, they failed. Beck was allowed to commit suicide but only managed to wound himself severely; he had to be shot instead. Von Stauffenberg was also shot and Goerdeler was hanged. Himmler was put in charge of rounding up the plotters: 7,000 people were arrested and almost 6,000 of them were executed. Some of those who were executed, such as von Stauffenberg's brother, were hanged with piano wire.

ACTIVITY

Do you think things would have been very different in Germany if Hitler had been killed in the 1944 Bomb Plot? Explain why you think this.

THE EXTENT OF OPPOSITION TO THE NAZIS

It is very difficult to judge how much of a threat the Nazis faced from opposition to their rule. Propaganda suggested everyone loved the government and any acts of opposition were not publicised. We know that there was resistance to Nazi policies from, for example, the Churches, the Communists, the Jews, the youth movements and the trade unions. What we don't know is how much support there was amongst the general population for such opposition.

The growth in membership of the Nazi Party, and its success in elections, suggests that Nazi rule was very popular in the early years, as it dealt with problems caused by the Depression. However, that support declined as the war began to go badly and there were shortages and hardships in the towns and cities. For example, in October 1944 there was an uprising in Cologne against Gestapo and Nazi officials which resulted in dozens of Germans being publicly hanged. However, it seems much more likely that, despite the fact that there were 11 attempts on Hitler's life, the opposition to the Nazis was not a real threat to their rule. Some Nazi policies, such as euthanasia, did lead to protest but the Nazi regime was strong enough to deal with this. It may well be that opposition to Nazi rule was seen more in 'the little things', such as absenteeism from work (in December 1941 over 7,000 workers were arrested for not attending work), buying on the black market and failing to report anyone seen to be opposing Nazi policies.

THE END OF THE THIRD REICH

By 1945, Germany was close to defeat. Allied forces were advancing on Germany from the west and the Soviet Red Army was approaching from the east (see Figure 5.3). To make matters worse, the Allies increased their bombing of German cities. The German troops fought bravely and it is believed that more soldiers died in the last 4 months of the war than in the whole of 1942 and 1943 put together. Huge numbers of refugees fled the cities to avoid the bombing or the advancing Red Army in the east. Up to a million civilians died from hunger, disease and cold.

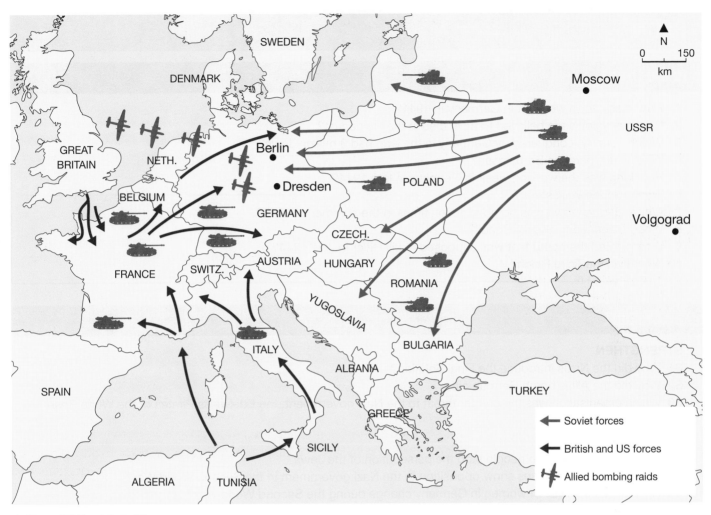

▲ **Figure 5.3** The defeat of Germany

On 28 April, Hitler married his long-time girlfriend, Eva Braun. Two days later, he shot himself and Eva took her own life with cyanide. Hitler left the control of Germany to Admiral Doenitz, who surrendered to the Allies on 7 May 1945. The Third Reich had come to an end.

RECAP

RECALL QUIZ

1 How many Jews were left in Germany in 1941?
2 How many Jews are believed to have died in the Holocaust?
3 Which country, conquered by Germany in the war, had 3 million Jews?
4 What was Operation Barbarossa?
5 How long was the working week in Germany in late 1944?
6 What was the *Volkssturm*?
7 Which German town was bombed seven times in the summer of 1943?
8 What happened to Sophie Scholl?
9 Who planted the bomb that was supposed to kill Hitler in July 1944?
10 What was the Third Reich?

CHECKPOINT

STRENGTHEN

S1 Why did the Nazis introduce the Final Solution?
S2 Why did the Allies bomb German cities?
S3 Which organisation was the greater threat to the Nazi government, the Edelweiss Pirates or the White Rose Group?

CHALLENGE

C1 Why didn't the German people stop the persecution of the Jews?
C2 Why did so few Germans show opposition to the Nazi government in the Second World War?
C3 How far did the lives of women in Germany change during the Second World War?

SUMMARY

■ When the Germans first conquered territory in Europe, they forced the Jews to live in ghettos.
■ In 1942, the Germans introduced the Final Solution.
■ The Germans made propaganda films to disguise what they were doing.
■ The Germans introduced rationing during the Second World War.
■ The German invasion of the Soviet Union proved to be a major mistake.
■ In September 1943, Goebbels announced that Germany was now in 'total war'.
■ Labour shortages meant that more women had to work during the war.
■ Allied bombing killed more than 600,000 German civilians.
■ A number of different protest groups started among young German people.
■ There was an attempt to blow up Hitler in 1944.
■ Hitler committed suicide in April 1945.
■ Germany surrendered in May 1945.

EXAM GUIDANCE: PART (A) QUESTIONS

Study Extract A.

From a modern history website.

You cannot expect to find a written record where Hitler has said 'Right, I'm taking the decision here and now to exterminate the Jews.' It just simply didn't work like that, but Hitler's fingerprints are all over all the anti-Jewish policy. And also, when it comes to all the crucial steps, such as deporting the Jews from Germany to the East, these could not be taken without Hitler's authorisation. Also, the yellow star on the sleeve of German Jews from September 1940 couldn't happen unless Hitler approved of it.

Hitler has been speaking throughout his whole career about the need to destroy the Jews, so we should not believe that the anti-Jewish policy could happen without him knowing about it, approving of it and authorising it.

Question to be answered: What impression does the author give about Hitler's role in the treatment of Jews?

You must use Extract A to explain your answer. (6 marks)

A04

SKILLS ANALYSIS, INTERPRETATION, CREATIVITY

1 **Analysis Question 1: What is the question type testing?**
In this question, you have to analyse the extract and work out what impression the author set out to create. The key to answering this type of question is to understand that the author deliberately chooses how they write. They will make a choice about the language they use, the tone they adopt and the content they include to create a particular impression.

2 **Analysis Question 2: What do I have to do to answer the question well?**
You need to read the extract carefully and work out what the author is trying to make you think. Has the author set out to give a positive or negative impression? Are they trying to suggest that an event or policy was significant or insignificant, successful or unsuccessful, and so on?

3 **Analysis Question 3: Are there any techniques I can use to make it very clear that I am doing what is needed to be successful?**
This is a 6-mark question and you need to make sure you leave enough time to answer the other two questions fully (they are worth 24 marks in total). This is not an essay and you don't need to give a general introduction or conclusion. All you need to do is answer the question as quickly as you can.

A good way to do this is to state your answer straight away – for example: 'The impression the author is giving about Hitler and the Jews is…'

Now you have to prove what you have said. You can do this by quoting from the answer, for example:
- 'I think this because of the language and tone…', then quote from the extract to prove what you are saying about language and tone.
- 'I also think this because of the content the author has chosen…', then quote from Extract A to prove what you are saying about content choice. For example, '…the author makes Hitler's role seem important as he says "Hitler's fingerprints are all over the main steps".'

Answer A

The author of Extract A gives the impression that Hitler had total control over the treatment of the Jews. His tone is very definite and he challenges the idea that Hitler might not have known what was going on. His language is very clear about Hitler and he gives examples of how Hitler must have had knowledge and given his authority and approval.

What are the strengths and weaknesses of Answer A?

Answer A does consider the tone, language and content of the extract and it provides some basic explanation. However the answer does not give specific examples or quote from the extract to support the points that have been made.

Answer B

The author of Extract A gives the impression that Hitler had total control over the treatment of the Jews. He is keen to challenge the idea that Hitler may not have known about what was really happening. He says that 'crucial steps... simply could not be taken' unless Hitler himself ordered them. His tone is very definite and he makes a clear argument by saying that Hitler had spent his whole life wanting the Jews destroyed, so it is not believable that he was not key to the holocaust. His language is very clear about Hitler. He says 'we should not believe' that the anti-Jewish measures happened without Hitler 'authorising it'. He also gives examples of how Hitler must have known what was going on because it says that Hitler's 'fingerprints were all over it'. The tone here is very definite.

What are the strengths and weaknesses of Answer B?

This is an excellent answer. It identifies and explains the tone, language and content in the extract. The answer includes specific quotes and examples taken directly from the extract.

Challenge a friend

Choose an extract from the Student Book and use it to set a part (a) question for a friend. Then look at the answer. Does it do the following things?

☐ State a valid impression from the extract
☐ Provide 3–4 lines explaining how language, tone and content choice prove this.

If it does, you can tell your friend that the answer is very good!

GLOSSARY

abortion a medical operation to end a pregnancy

alcoholic someone who is addicted to alcohol and cannot stop drinking

anti-establishment against the establishment or established authority

anti-Semitism hatred of the Jewish people

autarky a policy in which a country or area does not want or need goods, food, etc. from any other country or area

authoritarian strictly forcing people to obey a set of rules or laws

bankruptcy the state of being unable to pay your debts

bodyguard a person or group of people whose job is to protect an important person

campaign a series of actions intended to achieve a particular result relating to politics or business, or a social improvement

capitalism a way of running the economy (or a country) where individuals own businesses, fund them and take the profits from them

Catholic connected with the Roman Catholic Church (a part of the Christian Church whose leader is the Pope)

chancellor the leader of the government or the main government minister of some countries

Christian a person who believes in the ideas taught by Jesus Christ

citizenship the legal right of belonging to a particular country

civil servant someone employed in the civil service (the government departments that manage the affairs of a country)

coal mining digging coal out of the ground

colony a country or area that is under the political control of a more powerful country

conservative not liking changes or new ideas

contraception methods used to prevent a woman from becoming pregnant when she has sex

corruption dishonest, illegal, or immoral behaviour, especially from someone with power

deport make someone leave a country and return to the country they came from, especially because they do not have a legal right to stay

dictatorship a country which is run by a dictator (someone who rules a country using harsh or extreme methods)

diplomatic dealing with people politely and skilfully without upsetting them, particularly during political negotiations

emigration the process of leaving your own country and going to live in another one

empire a group of countries that are all controlled by one ruler or government

ethnic relating to a particular race, nation, or tribe and their customs and traditions

evacuate send people away from a dangerous place to a safe place

execution when someone is killed, especially as a legal punishment

extermination killing large numbers of people or animals of a particular type so that they no longer exist

extremist someone who has extreme political opinions and aims, and who is willing to do unusual or illegal things in order to achieve them

gas chambers large rooms in which people are killed with poisonous gas

gassed poisoned or killed with gas

ghettoisation a policy of forcing certain people to live in ghettos

graffiti rude, humorous, or political writing and pictures on the walls of buildings, trains, etc.

guillotine a piece of equipment used to cut off the heads of criminals

Gypsies a group of people who traditionally live and travel around in caravans, and who now live all over the world

hereditary passed from parent to child

homosexual sexually attracted to people of the same sex

Jews people whose religion is Judaism, or who are a member of a group whose traditional religion is Judaism

juvenile delinquent a child or young person who behaves in a criminal way

left wing a left-wing person or group supports the political aims of groups such as Socialists and Communists

lethal injection an injection used to kill someone, as a means of capital punishment

memorial something, especially a stone with writing on it, that reminds people of someone who has died

middle class the social class that includes people who are educated and work in professional jobs, for example teachers or managers

oath a formal and very serious promise

Pope the leader of the Roman Catholic Church

Protestant a member of a part of the Christian Church that separated from the Roman Catholic Church in the 16th century

purity the quality or state of being pure

radical radical ideas are very new and different, and are against what most people think or believe

rationing government restriction of how much food or other goods people can buy

raw materials substances that are used to make other products

rearm obtain weapons again or provide someone else with new weapons

rearmament increasing armed forces and weapons to restore a country's military strength

referendum when people vote in order to make a decision about a particular subject, rather than voting for a person

regime a government

resistance fighting against someone who you disagree with

right wing a right-wing person or group supports the ideas and beliefs of capitalism

Roman Catholic belonging or relating to the part of the Christian religion whose leader is the Pope

salute (n) an act of raising your right hand (for example, to your head) as a sign of respect, usually done by a soldier to an officer

Socialists people who believe in socialism, or are a member of a political party that supports socialism

speculation when you try to make a large profit by buying goods, property, shares, etc. and then reselling them at a higher price

sterilise if a person is sterilised, they have an operation to stop them producing babies

stormtrooper a member of a special group of German soldiers (the *Sturmabteilung* or SA) in the Second World War

Stosstrupp 'Shock Troop'; Hitler's own personal bodyguard

swastika a sign consisting of a cross with each end bent at a 90° angle, used as a sign for the Nazi Party in Germany

synagogue a building where Jewish people meet for religious worship

tactics methods used to achieve something

takeover the act of getting control of a country or political organisation, using force

torture the act of deliberately hurting someone in order to force them to tell you something, to punish them, or to be cruel

totalitarian a totalitarian state is one in which the government controls all aspects of life

treason the crime of being disloyal to your country or its government, especially by helping its enemies or trying to remove the government using violence

withdraw leave a place

INDEX